TRAVELS IN MOROCCO

By

Finbarr Corkery

Published by
     Ragworth press © 2017

Email: finbcorkery@hotmail.com

Contents.

Part 1: winter/spring 1979/80

                                                    Chapters 1-5

Part 2: winter 1992/93

                                                    Chapters 1-3

Part 3: summer 1994

                                                    Chapters 1-3

Part 4: 3 fortnights
      Chapter 1: spring 2007
      Chapter 2: spring 2014
      Chapter 3: autumn 2015

Travels in Morocco.

Part 1.

Winter/Spring 1979/80.

Entered Morocco on January 23rd and exited on May 8th.

Chapter 1.

I travelled through Spain early in 1980 on my way to Morocco in a VW van in company with Paddy, an ex- French legionnaire originally from the west of Ireland but then mostly resident in the east of England; Hannah, a puppet-maker from the midlands of England and her two infant sons, Chawakee and Blueberry; Stan, a rotund, giant street vendor from Norfolk in the east of England, and Karl (aka Carlos), the driver and owner of the van, who was the son of a nazi fugitive who had settled in Chile after the end of the second world war.
****

I left Ireland in late 1979 with Paddy, Hannah and her two sons in Paddy's estate wagon, which had a dozen thirty foot long pine tepee poles held in place on its roof by ropes tied to the front bumper and rear fender. We boarded a ferry in Rosslare in the south-east corner of Ireland bound for Wales and, immediately after disembarking, drove into the mountains to a place called Tepee valley, near to a village called Tally. There we found a community of people living side-by-side in tepees pitched in a field surrounded by craggy, mossy, mist-soaked, magic mushroom speckled slopes. There was even a temple-tepee which was twice as large as the other tepees and served as a prayer house where "the vic" conducted ceremonies for the community.

Paddy's original intent in visiting the place had been to pitch his tepee there for a few days to soak up the atmosphere, but to tell the truth the atmosphere was more akin to a tented council estate than a free-living, all-for-one-one-for-all, mine-is-yours-and-yours-is-mine, tribal gathering, as raggedy boys trailed me and my company, looking for handouts as they conducted us on an unofficial tour of the site.

The inhabitants of the tepees were a sour, unwelcoming lot, particularly the women, who slouched about in mud-caked ill-fitting garments, their long faces portraying their discomfort as they rattled fire-blackened kettles and pots and growled impatiently at snotty nosed, fright-eyed children. For all the world it seemed like the residents of Tepee Valley were attempting to recreate third-world conditions in the middle of Wales. I was amazed that people were deliberately encouraging their children to behave in a third-world fashion, hassling and begging from strangers and no doubt watching for a chance to pilfer from them. Tepee Valley was in reality a kind of refuge for fake tribalists; gaunt-faced, vacant-eyed escapees from city slums and heroin-nourished, fallen-from-grace, pseudo-hippy suburbanites.
****

I was glad to leave "Hackney-in-the-mountains" behind as Paddy steered a course for the Severn bridge, which took us into England. We stayed in a squat in Bristol for about a week before heading on to London, where I managed to find a room in a squat in a run-down housing estate off the Brecknock Road near Tufnell Park, north of the river Thames.

The other inhabitants were a dodgy bunch of junkies, creepy couples practising to be even creepier in their cocooned self-importance and various transient, shadowy, "lost souls". I did, however, manage to hook up with an "away-with-the-fairies" vagabond called "American Bob", who accompanied me on a beat up old guitar as I blew on a tin whistle while busking in cavernous, echoing underground tunnels.

On new year's eve night we found a pitch in Leicester Square underground station and managed to amass a tidy sum contributed by revellers in various degrees of euphoria before heading out to join the hordes gathered in Trafalgar Square. A new year was upon me and I was still stuck in England, even though the original plan on leaving Ireland had been to stay in England for as short a time as possible, pick up a decent sized van and head for the continent.

****

About a week into 1980 Paddy, myself, Hannah, her two sons and Stan, who had journeyed down from Norwich to join us, finally bade a glad farewell to Blighty as we boarded a hydrofoil in Ramsgate bound for Calais in France. We were travelling in a roomy, Ford Transit van, which was chock full of bags of food purchased at a shop in North London called "The Bumblebee", including sealed plastic bags containing dried fruit and nuts, bags of flour, rice and oatmeal and a large can of olive oil.

The van looked like a giant mobile T from the side with the top horizontal line of the T, consisting of the elongated bundle of the tepee poles, extending out in front and behind, while inside the tepee cover was stored in a compartment above the driver. Shortly after disembarking from the hovercraft in Calais, a gendarme motioned to Paddy to pull over to the side of the road, no doubt hoping to discover some punishable illegalities, but the sight of such a strange looking company of travelling companions crammed into a vehicle along with such an untidy jumble of belongings seemed to put him off and he waved us on very quickly.

Paddy drove in the direction of Paris and veered off towards the south before reaching the city centre. The route took us towards Beaujolais country in the mountains of the Massif Central, where I looked forward to sampling the local wines on the way through. However, our's was not to be a fleeting visit as our "Argo" foundered on the rocks of the Massif.

Paddy had neglected to check the oil properly, so the engine seized and we were stuck in the town of Macon, shivering inside the clapped-out van as snow fell outside or walking hurriedly along the banks of the Saone river, stopping occasionally at bars to drink glasses of cheap, full-bodied, red wine. Was this to be the end of our dream journey into Europe and beyond into Morocco? Everyone was agreed that it shouldn't be, and we resolved to continue forwards into Spain by whatever means that might present themselves. There was no going back!

******

We all agreed to meet up, if possible at all, at a bar in Castellon De La Plana, which is near Valencia on the Mediterranean coast, though blue seas and palm-lined beaches seemed a long way from our snowy, mountainy present stuck-place.

I travelled on alone, hoping to hitch-hike my way to the rendezvous point, hoping that the others would reach it in good time. As luck would have it, I didn't have to wait too long for a lift as a lorry drew into the side of the road to pick me up. Unfortunately, the driver was only going as far as Lyons, but it was a start and I was just happy to be able to make some progress on my journey.

That night I slept fitfully under a bridge opposite a hypermarket and the next day I continued on my way bright and early, shivering in the cold, damp, wintry air as I tried to make myself look a bit less bedraggled by smoothing the wrinkles from my clothes and unruffling my unkempt hair. Luck was with me that day as I got a lift from a lorry driver, who was travelling all the way to Barcelona; and so we journeyed on, through hilly, pine-clad countryside, past terracotta coloured slopes that contrasted with fleeting glimpses of a cobalt blue sea backdrop.

We had to wait for a while at the frontier while the driver went through the necessary formalities pursuant to gaining entrance to Spain, but it wasn't long before we were on our way again. The road climbed into the snow-covered Pyrenees before descending again on its way to Barcelona, where I thanked the driver for his assistance as I got off near the town centre. I strode down a palm-lined ocean

boulevard, happy to be caressed by a warm breeze from the Mediterranean, happy to leave snow and ice behind, but still driven on by a sense of urgency as I wanted to make sure that I reached Castellon as soon as possible. I made my way to the highway going south and managed to persuade a trucker at a motorway café to take me as far as Castellon, where I found the bar-rendezvous point in a backstreet. Unfortunately, it was closed and, by the looks of it, hadn't been open for some time. Though somewhat taken aback by the discovery, I didn't panic and I decided to head for the town centre in the hope of bumping into my original travelling companions, wondering if they too were looking for me at the same time.
****

My relief was great when I finally found most of them sitting on benches in the train station, where Hannah was trying to coax her sons into sleeping bags that lay on the floor. Seemingly, she, her sons and Stan had journeyed all the way by bus. Paddy stayed behind alone and hitched, hoping to carry as much of the stuff from the broken down van as he possibly could along with him. He thought the poles were too unwieldy for most people's liking, so he found a lorry driver who was willing to take them back to England.

Karl, who was travelling from Germany on his way to Spain in his VW van pulled in when he saw Paddy's beckoning thumb. He offered to take Paddy along with a load of gear as far as Castellon in Spain and beyond to Andalusia. Paddy gratefully accepted and, as they travelled on, tried to persuade Karl to consider going over the sea to Morocco, promising money for fuel and other expenses as an incentive.

Soon after I met up with Hannah, Karl and Paddy arrived at the train station, where we all expressed pleasure at our successful reconnection. The following day, we headed south to Valencia and onwards into the mountains, where we set up camp near a little village called Alcalali. There, I swallowed a few magic mushrooms gathered from fields in the Boggeragh mountains in the south-west of Ireland before wandering about among orange groves that were watered by a fast-flowing, crystal-clear mountain stream. At one stage I was approached by an elderly man who, unbidden, presented me with some oranges that he'd freshly plucked from a tree nearby, and I gratefully accepted them before resuming my meanderings, peeling the soft, deep skin from an orange and sucking the sweetness from its bulbous flesh as I marvelled at the subtle colours being brought on by the approaching sunset.

As we were setting up camp, a local policeman arrived on the scene and was reassured by Karl, who spoke fluent Spanish, that we were just camping there for the night and would be gone by the next day. Who knows?; maybe the locals had some trouble in the past with other people camping in the area. Either way, the policeman seemed happy to let us stay where we were for the night and he went on his way again.

The next day, we headed off again through the mountains, past cave-homes whose presence was betrayed by wooden doors and little windows on the hill-sides and little villages with street stalls stacked with glazed ceramics; on through the scrubby, spaghetti-western landscape and into Andalucia, where we passed through the outskirts of Moorish Granada, whose Alhambra gardens are a world-renowned delight.
****

We left the mountains behind for a while as we visited the tourist towns of Torremolinos and Fuengirola on the Costa Del Sol, where we replenished dwindling food-stocks, mostly legally but partially by shop-lifting in the large supermarkets. I managed to purloin a sturdy dagger, which I slid into an inside pocket and was on the point of leaving the shop when I was accosted by a security guard, who demanded the return of the stolen item. I looked shocked for the guard's benefit before handing another knife, which was markedly inferior to the one I'd taken, to the waiting guard. On my way again, I promised myself that I'd be more careful in future, but in my heart I knew that desperation often wins out over clever intent, that hunger urges foolhardiness where heron-like patience would garner safe success, that needs must has a head start on biding one's time..

****

Karl suggested that we visit Castellar De La Frontera, a "white" village in the mountains behind the port of Algeciras, and so we wound our way through San Roque, past a slogan daubed on a roadside cliff, saying "hippie Allemanes go home", up past towering eucalyptus trees, stocky, fan-crowned pineapple palms, orange groves and sweet-scented, flowering, almond orchards, and into an ancient castle courtyard.

The view from the castle ramparts was stunning, extending from pine-clad mountains in the north down to the giant whale-rock of Gibraltar, whose frontier was temporarily closed to traffic coming from mainland Spain. The EEC didn't include Spain then but since it's accession the dispute over who should have control over the rock still rumbles on. Tensions have eased since Spain joined up for sure and people can travel easily between rock and mainland, but it may be a long time before Britain is prepared to negotiate away one of its prize relics of Empire. The "planted" inhabitants, somewhat like those of the Falkland Islands in the South Atlantic, are dyed-in-the-wool Union Jackers of course. Spain, meantime, jealousy holds on to its North African enclaves in Cueta and Melilla. I'm not sure if they'll be giving them back any time soon.

****

After a couple of days spent resting near the castle, it was time to take the next big step, i.e., the ferry to Morocco, and so we piled into the van again and descended into Algeciras, where we caught a ferry for Ceuta. We decided to stay within the environs of the Ceuta enclave for a night and drove up a coastal hill, where we found a spot to set up camp.

There, I went for a stroll further up the hill, pondering on the significance of the site, which, along with Gibraltar across the way, was reputed to be the location of a pillar of Hercules. In ancient times the pillars of Hercules stood guard, so myth has it, over the edge of the known world, affording the possessors a view over the portal provided by the Straits of Gibraltar into the Mediterranean. It was a key location along with the Bosphorus at the other end of the Mediterranean, one if held that offered unparalleled possibilities of commercial and military control.

My mythological musings were rudely interrupted, however, by a loud bang that seemed to have come from somewhere on the hill top and I warily strode on, looking around for the source. Suddenly, there in front of me was a group of Spanish soldiers gathered round a smoking, mobile canon, whose muzzle was pointing out to sea. I didn't feel like hanging about unsurprisingly, trying to protest my innocence in broken Spanish as I dug a deeper hole for myself while trying to reassure them that I wasn't on some spying mission, so I beat a hasty retreat back to camp.

The following day, we struck camp as a watercolour sun peeped over the eastern horizon and groped its way round and beyond Hercules's leaning-posts. We joined a queue of traffic that was waiting to cross over the border into Morocco. A Moroccan, you could say he was a sort of self-appointed tour guide, helped us by providing us with entry forms that needed to be completed and presented to the customs officers before crossing the border.

Chapter 2.

After a few hours delay, we finally crossed over into Morocco together with the "tour guide" and, much relieved to have made it into Morocco at last, there was an air of general euphoria in the van. Glad to see the backs of the armed-to-the-teeth Spanish and Moroccan border guards, we gazed in wonder as Karl's fiery chariot sped on to Tetouan. It was once the provincial capital of a Spanish Protectorate that was established in the early twentieth century but is now under the control of the Moroccan state, which was established in 1956.

As we passed through village clusters, trying to avoid rickety bicyclers, scrawny donkeys with overloaded carts in tow, jay-walking, djellabaed pedestrians and dare-devil hens, it felt like we were going back in time. Not far from the border in Ceuta, we came across a group of horse-riders, who looked like they'd come straight out of some Mediaeval tale, complete with billowing cloaks, blue, meringued turbans and hand-held muskets. I breathed a sigh of relief when our hitch-hiker guide told us that the unexpected cavalry was just a troop of travelling performers, who were on their way to a tourist venue. I should have guessed from his calm disposition that we were under no threat, but who knew if he was or wasn't in on the act? How long is it, after all, since slaves captured on raiding expeditions were held nearby? Some of them might even have been snatched from Baltimore in West Cork. Times change, yes, but not always for the better.

We stopped in Tetouan for a little while to have a stroll round. There, amongst bustling street markets, I marvelled at the surrounding mountain scenery that rose up from the ends of Andalusian-inspired avenues and held the town in its lap. Leaving Tetouan behind, we headed east towards the Mediterranean coast and then south onto a little used road through the Rif mountains. Our Moroccan passenger had assured us that it led past a farm where we could buy some locally cultivated marijuana (kif). Rolling hills stretched in towards the interior. Anyone looking to begin with would have thought that noone could have lived up there, but a more concentrated gaze led eyes towards well camouflaged, mud-walled and tin-roofed dwellings that could just about be discerned, stuck high on pine-speckled hilltops.

Once, when we stopped to stretch our legs, I looked on as a hooded figure led a donkey down a steep, scree-roughened slope and over a shallow, freezing, boulder-strewn mountain stream;

"now, there's a relaxed way of life, far from the rat-race and subject only to natural rhythms", I'd thought to myself as I watched man and beast make their way over the road and onto a footpath that seemed to lead to nowhere.

****

A rocky track off the main road brought us to the promised farm. There we were greeted by a middle-aged, sunburnt, woollen-capped man, who invited us to come into his humble, adobe house. He motioned to us to sit down while his wife brewed up some refreshing mint tea, which she served up in glass tumblers that were crammed with fist-sized sugar-boulders and garnished with floating sprigs of dark-green, aromatic, fresh mint. We tore round loaves of bread to bits and dipped them in cold-pressed olive oil that had been poured into a bowl. It seems somehow biblical looking back on it now, what with the breaking of bread and anointing with oil, Hercules's oil even seeing as he is closely associated with his olive-wood staff.

The analogy can stop there, I think, since we didn't, as far as I know, transubstantiate any foods or drinks nor seek to memorialise such mutations. Instead, Paddy managed to buy several ounces of good quality grass, a substance that many of the transsubstantiators link automatically with the word "abuse". The bread and wine may turn into the body and blood of a deity in their imaginations, a deity who is promptly horribly dispatched while being commemorated. Marijuana has no such connotations, but does it lead to questioning? Have I asked one?

Curiously, without warning, our host interrupted his negotiations with Paddy so he could say his prayers to Allah. He just stopped as if in mid-sentence, turned round and went to fetch his prayer mat. Maybe, he was consulting his creator in his own mind, or was he trying to show Him that he was still His servant despite having to trade with infidels. The farmer's Islamic pillar didn't come crashing down, so he must have assumed that Allah wasn't too bothered.

As we were leaving, one of the farmer's sons noticed my silver-coloured dagger and asked me for it, but I didn't want to give it to him and managed to fob him off with a gift of an unwanted item of clothing. My dagger was, in truth, a rather blunt instrument. The blade may have seemed sturdy and lethal at a quick glance, but a closer look could only have disappointed both assassins and chefs. Still, I'd felt the need to hang on to it, like some cowboy venturing into the wild west, forever checking his holster to make sure he can reach for his gun at all times.

****

We joined the main road south near Chefchaouen, which was almost exclusively closed to non-muslims up until the 1920s.

We made good time on the journey towards Marrakesh; through the frenetic town square in Ouezzane, on through the Frenchified main thoroughfare passing through the holy city of Fez; past the cedar suburbs of Azrou and the tapestry of rectangular orchards and grain-fields enclosed by statuesque, needle-like cypress trees that covers the plain near Beni-Mellal.

Beyond, we climbed up into the heights of the Middle Atlas mountains where spiny, bulbous, wild cacti gardens stretched all the way from mountain tops, overflowing onto roads that cut into the mountain-sides. As we journeyed on towards Marrakech, we usually looked for campsites off the main roads as sunset approached, preferring mountain tracks that led to tree-shady sites, which could provide both shelter from prying eyes and fallen branches to feed a camp fire. There, Paddy would balance the tepee cover on several make-do, found by the wayside poles, simultaneously tying ropes attached to the cover's bottom edge to small wooden stakes driven into the hard, stony ground.

When pitched, the tent looked like a giant golden butterfly that had alighted upon the ground or a life-sized nativity shrine, especially at night in the flickering firelight with a spot-bright planet perched above it in the vast sky. At one campsite high in the mountains, I wandered about in my bare feet, treading on snow pools that were being turned to steam by scorching sunrays right in front of my eyes. That place was like some natural triple-point where elemental solids, liquids and gases existed all at once. It was definitely a good place to convince anyone of the mutability of things.

Marrakech, our "Shangrila", welcomed us, or so it seemed as throngs of arms-outstretched date palms that provide a buffer between the city and the looming mountains waved us in.

****

The contrast between the serene open spaces of the Atlas mountains and the cramped mayhem that was Marrakech could hardly have been greater, but I soon got into the flow of city life as I wandered about in the central square, which is known as the ""Djemaa El Fnaa".

As I sipped some orange juice bought from one of the many mobile stalls ranged about the square, I immersed myself in the jumble of sights, sounds and smells that permeated the atmosphere. Circles of people were gathered round tumbling Berber boy acrobats, travelling minstrels bowing rudimentary violins and beating out rhythms on tan-tan drums, and aged storytellers who embellished their tales with exaggerated body language.

Mesmeric snake-charmers blew on swollen pipes as leaf-headed cobras swayed from side to side, all the while keeping a nervous eye on innocuous looking goatskin tambours on the ground beneath. The vigilance was necessary since coiled-up horned vipers lay trapped inside, venomous creatures that were likely to scare the BeMuhammad out of passing tourists who showed an interest in their shows.

I took the weight off my feet and sat down at a table on the footpath outside the Café de France, where I nursed a cup of coffee served up by a moustachioed waiter while casting an eye over the square that was dominated by the imposing, filigreed Koutubia Minaret. I visited its "twin" tower, the Tour Hassan in Rabat 12 years later. It was built around the same time in the late 1100s by the Almohad dynasty. Back in Ireland, monks were often forced to hide in round towers around then as marauding Vikings stole what they could from the settlements outside. The Moroccan towers have a Norman look about their shapes, oddly enough, while the Irish ones seem more Egyptian.

Opposite the Café de France, a gate led into a market (souk) maze, where avenues of stalls criss-crossed each other, stretching into seeming infinity. Details from a layered landscape came rapidly into focus and were just as rapidly reabsorbed by its tapestry; mounds of waxy-skinned dates, hanging necklaces of sugar-dusted, dried figs, trays of shelled, crunchy almonds and peanuts in charred-roasted shells, stacked canvas sacks opened at the top to reveal contents including maize seeds, wheat flour, oats, millet, broad beans, chick peas, lentils and rice.

Exotic scent-breezes drifted in the air and nose pointed eyes at spice trays and herb-racks overflowing with a painter's palette of colour; golden saffron-dunes, loamy-brown cumin-hills, crimson, chilli-volcano lava-streams, jet-black pepper-swamps and flecked-marble garlic-pyramids, surrounded by a variegated jungle of coriander, thyme and mint copses, cinnamon-bark woodpiles, and knobbly ginger tree-roots. Other avenues were lined with clothes shops that displayed colourful garments dangling on coat-hanger branches in a man-woven-leaved forest. Sometimes I came across stalls selling western-style, formal suits, standing alone amidst multitudes selling native costumes. I imagined that they looked like the answers to "odd-one-out" competitions that had strayed into a Berber tableau or onto a "Tales of Araby" film set.

An apothecary's stall proved to be a very odd Aladdin's cave with a curious mixture of objects, including bowls of cochineal, a dye harvested from beetles and used as a lip-gloss, of powdered, aqua-marine, crystalline, kohl eye-shadow, of pulverised henna powder, which is used as a base for natural tattoos, and trays crammed with strips of tooth-cleaning walnut bark and marble-sized, nodular oak-apples, which are reputed to be a remedy against gastric problems when crushed and ingested. A shelf inside was stacked with glass jars containing pickled lizards, coiled snakes and button-topped, dried, opium poppy-heads. Stranger still was a bag stood in a corner of the shop, overflowing with a melange of feathers, bits of plastic, snail shells and various other puzzling bits and pieces It was like a collection a magpie might amass to decorate its nest, I thought, though I guessed that the bizarre jumble was meant to be

used when attempting to invoke supernatural assistance for the purpose of casting spells and appeasing deities.
****

After a sojourn of a couple of days in Marrakech, we left town and headed up into the High Atlas Mountains on a route that led towards the ocean. A lone cyclist flagged the van down in a middle-of-nowhere place that was coveted by the shifting sands of the greedy Sahara desert. We all thought he was either in some distress or, maybe just looking for a ride, possibly because of a puncture, but much to our surprise, he rolled up a sleeve of his djellaba and motioned to us to inspect the plastic-strapped watches clasped on his arm. All that way to buy a plastic watch in a place where the sun could melt it into a Dali grotesque at noon! Maybe the watch-seller was a figment of the imagination, perhaps acting in surreal time.

Cacti whorls clung to the mountainsides like giant green snowflakes nestling together on ice-gouged, Bangor roof-slates as Karl drove cautiously along the looping, hairpin-bended road, being particularly careful to stay clear of edges that bordered sheer drops that descended to valleys hundreds of feet below. We climbed up to and over the high mountain pass at Tizi'n Test and then descended into the Souss valley. We skirted the walled town of Taroudant and eventually caught a first sight of the Atlantic and Agadir.

It appeared like a mirage, spread out along the dazzling, blue Atlantic's coast. I swear I can remember the collective gasp that greeted the first views of the sea, whose whoosh must have whispered in response, inviting the thirsty desert deserters to slake their thirsts in the biggest trough ever.

Chapter 3.

Agadir was hit by a devastating earthquake in 1961 and, consequently, the town centre boasts an array of modern buildings and plazas that were constructed as part of a redevelopment plan. There you can see hordes of tourists, promenading, shopping, eating and drinking, surrounded by palm trees, spongy-to-the-touch, aloe-vera spikes, giant, raspy, mother-in-law's-tongue slats and blood-red-flowering, bougainvillea lawns.
An inquiry about suitable campsites nearby led us north along the coast to the village of Tarhazoute, which straddles cliffs bordering on sandy beaches that stretch between dark, mussel-encrusted, basalt rock-barriers and are washed by regularly-breaking, six-foot waves. The journey out of Agadir took us past docks crammed with trawlers that were offloading sardines destined for canning factories, on past a camping-gas extraction plant and a cement works, through Banana village, where street-side stalls were hung with clusters of the local dwarf variety of bananas, and, just a few hundred yards before Tarhazoute proper, down a lane which led to a beach area serviced by a campsite, a shop and a couple of restaurants.
Karl drove onto the beach and steered away from the village towards a collection of sand-dunes, where we set up camp, perching the tepee cover on a single central pole that was made up of two poles lashed together and tying it to stakes driven deep into the sand. The tent was protected by sand-dunes on the windward side and weighted with rocks placed on the cover's edges as a further safety measure against wind-induced collapse.
At long last we'd arrived and noone felt like going a step further, but for how long no one knew for sure, since money was scarce, and any thoughts of returning to England or Ireland were buried beneath desires to savour the momentary situation. After all, looking on the bright side, there was the great weather and so many of the best things in life are free, the delights of beachcombing for instance, and rock-pool gazing, invigorating sea-bathing and campfire-side dining on hunter-gathered seafoods beneath a starry sky.
Besides, as the saying much quoted by the Furry Freak brothers in their comics goes, "grass (hash in our case) will get you through times of no money better than money will get you through times of no grass". It definitely helps you to savour the moment, to stop you reaching for that never quite attainable object of desire. I suppose you could say it has a tranquillising effect, but not a deadening one. It certainly tends to take people out of themselves, or what they think they are, and helped me to acclimatise and appreciate my new surroundings; the golden beaches, the rocky, shell-strewn paths, the argan-tree-covered slopes and the narrow village lanes that centred on a square lined with little blue shops.
Stan, the Norfolk giant, had no wish to stay on in Tarhazoute, particularly since money resources were depleting fast. The spectre of starvation must have loomed large for such a large appetite, but if it did then it was well hidden behind his elephant-seal-proportioned frame when he decided to take a dip in the ocean. His self-ducking was like some comedy routine in truth as he stripped to the waist and wrapped a blanket round his body before immersing himself in a gently breaking wave. Then, just as quickly, he ploughed his way back out again on to dry land.
That seemingly was the pilgrimage-completed point of his journey, the kissed-the-Blarney-stone, met-the-Pope-in-Rome, circled-round-the-Kaaba, plucked-the-golden-apple moment to be catalogued and invested with importance by his memory. Just like pilgrims everywhere afterwards who've done their "duty", he'd had enough of

discomfort and foreign food and wished only to return home as soon as possible. Luckily for him, he managed to hook up with a van heading north to Spain and beyond, but I didn't envy him one bit his chance to return home even though all I had in the world was about thirty pounds sterling and the raggedy clothes I was wearing. Life settled into a pleasant rhythm for a while as there were still some food supplies left and a little money for daily necessities to be satisfied as well as plenty good quality hash, which is worth its weightlessness in calm introspection.

Mornings I liked to stroll along the beach near the water's lapping edge, past statuesque groups of wading birds and cotton-bowl-capped matchstick fishermen, paddling small clinker-built, wooden boats through overarching waves and out to sea. Sometimes I was lucky enough to meet fishermen returning with their day's catch of sardines, crabs, lobsters and even octopi and it wasn't difficult to persuade one to sell me some sea-food cheap, thus augmenting camp provisions with nutritional fare. Usually, my treks led past a seaside shop, where, if I had any money, I sometimes bought some breakfast goodies, including bundles of large-leaved, refresh-smelling mint, freshly baked, elongated, French-style baguettes, round wholemeal loaves of Moroccan bread, dark-ochre-pigmented, free-range eggs, slabs of butter cut from a block and wrapped in Arabic script newspaper and large, fleshy, succulent oranges or sweet-melting-membraned tangerines. Occasionally I bought some dinner stuff as well, including half-litre plastic bottles of black olive oil and fresh vegetables.

It was a real treat, if you could afford it, to sample the locally produced argan-tree oil, which is processed from berries that have passed through the digestive systems of goats, which could often be seen perched precariously on the thorny branches of hill-hugging argan trees. Once, when I tasted some of the oil, I noticed that it had a flavour of almonds tempered with sunflower seeds.

An official campsite near the shop contained a motley clientele of Germans, English and French for the most part, who had travelled there in dream-machine campervans, though for some their dreams seemed to be fading along with their dwindling resources. It wasn't too difficult to see who were having better social lives, since the ones who were always at home day or night obviously didn't have any social life at all.

Once, when I asked a tourist in the nearby village if he knew where I could buy some hash, he invited me to follow him to a rented room, where I was introduced to a shady, menacing-looking Frenchman, who accused me of being English and therefore, in his eyes, below contempt. I, as soon as I'd blurted out a denial of my alleged nationality, felt like saying "fuck you, Josephine! Not tonight! Not toujours!", but instead made my excuses and left the "sans-culottes" behind to stew in his man-the-barricades, off-with-their-heads, marseillaise-bawling misery.

It must have been difficult for French tourists at times, I think, trying, if they weren't too stupid, not to incite loathing as colonials who had occupied Morocco up until as recently as a quarter of a century before, but the majority of them didn't help matters by their aloof manners and haughty demeanour towards the natives. I noticed furthermore that there seemed to be at least three different types of French tourist holidaying in the locality, i.e., working-class refugees from justice or army conscription, particularly from the far-reaching claws of the French Foreign Legion; tight bands of done-army-service, young men who followed rigid time-tables, rising at dawn to studiously plan out the activities of each day and above all seeing to the proper maintenance of their vehicles; and middle-aged or beyond sun-seekers, who were generally the easiest to get along with of the lot.

Paddy's tepee attracted a mixture of down-at-heel, beach-stranded people like Rodolfo from Holland and Kumal from Casablanca, who ended up sleeping and eating there even though they never seemed to contribute anything. A Moroccan named Brahim, who said he was an ex-army captain, often dropped by for a chat around the fire at night under the starlit heavens. It wasn't hard to imagine that he was on some sort of spying mission, possibly searching for any information about terrorist attacks planned against soft tourist targets by "Polisario" agents.

Rumours had it, possibly ones publicised by the King's men themselves to create public unease and heighten paranoia, that Polisario terrorists/freedom-fighters had travelled across the border from the neighbouring country of Western Sahara with evil intents. Morocco had only recently tried to annexe their lands with the aid of rhetoric-driven citizens, who were promised lands as a reward for Green-Marching into territories that were not theirs by right.

Captain Brahim was, unsurprisingly, circumspect in his choice of themes, I mean he gave the bush a good beating round, inquiring in mostly general ways about our origins and plans and saying little about his own. He was a genial man though and liked to laugh and joke, but I wouldn't have risked making fun of King Hassan, not like I might have done in Queen Elizabeth's case for Hannah's benefit. The captain's affability may have been a mask to disguise his true mission, I know, but I realised that his goodwill could help to keep the authorities away from us, especially those of us running out of funds or just plain broke. Later, in Casablanca, I met him again to my great surprise. He gave me some advice then which I should have listened to, I know now.

On Tarhazoute beach he often stayed till very late, maybe, now that I think of it, because he didn't want to go back to some cramped, overpopulated cell-room in the pokey village. I often saw him looking up at the stars and down into driftwood embers glowing on the golden sand. Maybe, he was wondering who was spying on him.

The burying of the embers usually called time on discussions and visitors either drifted away or joined us in Paddy's tepee where Hannah often coaxed embers retrieved from their sandy graves back into life in a terracotta brazier. As soon as they began to glow again, she used to throw some bits of sweetly smoking driftwood and finger-pinches from a bag of incense purchased at a souk on top. Incense, sandalwood, cedar, pine, scents would permeate the atmosphere inside the tepee, calming and sleep-inducing.

****

One morning, when I needed to relieve myself I crawled out of the tepee and was surprised to see a large Mercedes van parked just a few yards away. Not long after, the van's inhabitants came calling and introduced themselves as Franz, his wife Frieda, their blond son Otto and their Alsatian guard-dog, Max, all the way from Germany.

It was a timely arrival, since, as Karl had returned to Spain in his van, we had no transport to convey us to markets and such like places. Pleading impending destitution, Paddy persuaded Franz and his companions to team up with us to put on a show for whatever contributions we could coax out of spectators. He had heard, he said, about a huge weekly market that was well within reach, just a few miles south of Agadir in a satellite town called Inezgane. Truth was, they were nearly as broke as us and that was why they hadn't parked up in the official campsite. Insecurity had led them to park near us, a happy accident for us you might think, but they also benefited. Thursday, market day, came round and we all piled into Franz's van and headed for Inezgane. There Franz strummed a guitar, accompanying myself and Hannah. We gadded about, pretend dancing with hand held, almost life-sized puppets inside a circle of local people, at the same time encouraging a couple of the bigger children to hold out upturned tambours in front of the spectators, looking for contributions. Paddy became the star of the show for a few moments when his fire-breathing act went badly awry. His jet propulsion must have stuttered or a puff of wind may have blown fuel back on to his face, who knows? Either way, his beard caught fire, not a happy accident you should say, nor a cause for humour, but that didn't stop the laughter, which began somewhat nervously. It became louder when Paddy began to howl as he patted his face violently in an attempt to put the fire out. Unsurprisingly, he didn't choose to repeat his fire-eating performance after that day.

Though the day's takings were small enough, foodstuffs were so cheap in the souk that the little money we made helped us to supplement decreasing provisions, hopefully detaining the wolf-at-the-door until the next performance at least. After the show I went off by myself to check out stalls ranged along bustling avenues, stopping along the way in a swallow-swept square to pat a tied-up horse that promptly gave me a nasty nip for my troubles.

"There's gratitude!", I'd thought, as I quickly bade the horse goodbye before going on my way again, thinking, "with such an appetite for human flesh, surely I've just been bit by one of Diomedes's mares. Wasn't the flesh of Diomedes' guests enough for the brazen horse?".

The searing heat of the day sent me scurrying for shelter in a tin roofed, make-do restaurant, where wizened, old mountain Berbers sat on mats on the ground, sipping strong, sugar-loaded, mint tea poured into glass tumblers from little rose-motif teapots that were left to draw in metal charcoal burners. I joined the tea party, nervously eyeing the sugarberg that the teamaker was holding in his hand, hoping that I too wouldn't end up with a mouthful of silver teeth like corrugated-pewter shutters in tanned-lips window-frames.

Returning to Tarhazoute after the day's adventures, we'd seemed happy enough on the outside, at least a little less pessimistic about survival possibilities, but the forced-cheerfulness face-masks barely hid the general sense of a rising panic, simmering too closely for comfort below boiling point.

******

Back at the tepee, things went from bad to worse as an epidemic of dysentery struck, laying people low one after another, sending sufferers shuffling across shifting sands while holding their sides till the bowels could wait no more and liquid shit sprayed patterns in chocolate mousse flecked with blood on the undug sand. Paddy, Hannah, her two sons, Rodolfo, Kumal, Franz, Frieda, their son and myself were all afflicted, but, instead of diminishing morale, the plague brought people closer together. It made us realise that we only had each other to rely on and reinvigorated in us that much endangered spirit of survival, which is so lacking in the pampered citizens of the "first" world.

Hannah, a great believer in natural remedies, rummaged through some boxes till she found a bag of oak-apples, which she'd bought in an apothecary shop in Marrakech. She pounded some of the wasps' nests in a pestle before mixing the resultant paste with more palatable food, the better to persuade plague victims to eat up and swallow. The cure was too slow in coming, however, for some impatient patients, who were expecting some sort of instant respite from symptoms at the very least.

Paddy, ever the forward looking visionary, said he had just the thing for upset stomachs as he held up a bag of dried opium-poppy seed-heads. He explained that he'd bought the opium poppies in the same apothecary's shop that had provided them

with the oak-apples, sure in the knowledge that they would prove very useful in cases of gastric illness. He knew that there were few better constipatives and none that he knew of that had such a calming effect on patients.
He planned to administer the drug in tea form, doused in boiling water just like any other tea and brewed for a quarter of an hour or so in front of the fire. I gleefully accepted a cup of opium tea when offered, wishing an Aswan dam upon the floodtide Nile in my colonic canal. I wasn't disappointed as I didn't need to go shit for three days; three hazy, yellow, laying-about, parched-throated, cold-sweat-drenched, random- childhood-memories flash-backed, intermittently hash-becalmed days, and waking-dream nights haunted by ethereal shades and bathed by a moon surging/towing aethereal tide under the sway of the Herb of Forgetfulness.
I couldn't remember a thing so something must have worked, and I no longer felt like there was a volcano eager to erupt from my rear-end.
Rodolfo and Kumal also had their three day descents into hell and ensuing resurrections, a bit like Jesus I suppose, but we all only made it to the waiting-room. The rising didn't raise me up ("You raise me uuuuuuup!") to heaven either. God, I would have been dead then, killed by the cure. No thanks!
I'm glad to say that the opium tea, while it had its obvious curative properties, didn't become my regular beverage. As far as I can recall, it tended to drive people inwards, too far inwards in some cases, into curled-up womb-seekers. Rodolfo and Kumal wanted some more, however, presumably because they believed that they hadn't gone in far enough, nor risen high enough.
"Reality" was all too "real" for them it seems as they took to their beds for over a week, unsurprisingly swapping harsh contemporary realities for cushioned, cloud-cuckoo lands. Though grateful for the relief from painful symptoms provided by the opium tea and for its calming effect on frayed nerves, I nevertheless knew of its addictive reputation (who didn't?) and was wary of the cosy netherworld opium seemed to offer.
****
The ensuing full moon seemed to draw even more stragglers to the tepee's fireside, increasing pressures on already scarce food resources. After all, you couldn't deny starving people a morsel of food, especially when it could be your turn to be doing the begging soon. The night of the full moon saw a dozen people crammed underneath the tepee cover; me, Paddy, Hannah, Chawakee, Blueberry, the Captain, Kumal, Rodolfo, a young Brazilian couple (the girl was from the state of Amazonas) and a local teenage boy/girl couple who told us that they were on the run from parental persecution in their hometown, Immouzer in the Haut Atlas mountains above "Paradise Valley". It seems weird now that I think of it, that the refugees descended from on high down through "Paradise" to be with us in God know's where. He surely works in mysterious ways.
During the night the wind suddenly picked up and a mass of dark clouds moved across the sky, blotting out the face of the glowing moon as they unleashed a torrent of rain upon the Earth below. Three days the storm lasted, soaking everybody and everything in its wake and eroding bits off mountains that were carried as silt in mud-slides that flowed through almost dried-up river channels to the sea.
Incautious campers who had set up home near river-banks and in low-lying areas that attracted floods drained from higher areas were inundated, though luckily noone was drowned. All we could do during the storm was wait for it to end, sending out volunteers occasionally to brave the howling gales in search of food and water. When it eventually died down, Paddy said "let's move!" and Hannah and I had no objection.

We had few provisions left after all, and who knew when Mother Teresa would come spying, looking to see off the competition, us "heathen" poor-lovers.

We can't have loved them all that much since we neglected to tell Rodolfo and Kumal, our beloved brethren, that we were upping sticks. After three whole days being cooped up in a crowded tepee, even they wanted to get out and leave it behind for a while, enough of a while for us to make our escape in Franz's van.

*****

Franz turned right towards Agadir and then, after a few miles, right again down a desert track, which brought us to a sand-dune-sheltered site out of sight and, hopefully, out of reach of other down-on-their-luck travellers. We set up camp there for a few days and were just beginning to feel at home when raided by police. Happily, they weren't very thorough in their search for illegally held hash-stashes. I think they were just trying to intimidate us, maybe at the behest of a powerful landowner who wanted us out. They went through the motions anyway, rummaging through rucksacks and suitcases, in cardboard-box supply containers and under scattered blankets.

In times gone by, Agadir and its environs were part of what were termed "Dissident Lands (Bled El Siba). In fact most of Morocco, apart from the plains, Marrakech, Fez, Meknes, Rabat and some ports lay outside the "Governed Lands (Bled El Makhzen)". There, the sultans ruled, but Berber tribes had to be reckoned with on the outside. It reminds me some bit of the "Pale", that imaginary boundary between the British imperial city of Dublin and those "beyond the pale". Oddly enough, such a distinction still exists, only nowadays we're called "Culchies".

The dapper Moroccan policemen, with their well maintained uniforms and menacing holsters weren't going to stand for any of that anarchic stuff, it seemed. All were now "Governed" lands, and who was the "guvnor"? King Hassan II of course!

Whatever their authority or motives, they could find nothing incriminating in their search, so they left shortly after they arrived with their tails somewhat between their legs. Thankfully, they failed to discover our precious stash, which was buried in a hole in the ground beneath the tepee's ground-sheet under a carefully cut out sod of earth that was sprinkled with sand in an attempt to hide dig-lines.

Just as we were preparing to leave, a nervous looking American tourist showed up. Unsurprisingly, we were suspicious to begin with. His accent might have led us to believe under different circumstance that he was just another drifter who had wandered our way, but his curiously formal enquiries had us puzzled, particularly his request to be introduced to "our leader".

I asked "what leader?" and then added " We have no leader here. This isn't the damned army, you know", and Paddy concurred, castigat ing the intruder for making assumptions about hierarchical divisions existing within the campers' group structure. Happily, he only wanted to buy some hash, and Paddy obliged by selling him a little before sending him on his way again.

We left the site soon afterwards and headed for the souk in Inezgane. We badly needed provisions, particularly food and diesel and, of course, a new campsite, but that decision was left for later. Mind you, the label "desirable" when attached to "location" had recently acquired a new meaning for us. It no longer just evoked visions of sheltered places within easy reach of golden beaches and, possibly, near enough to useful shops. We also wanted some effective isolation, away from parasitic transients and harrassitic policemen.

The marketplace was exceptionally busy on the day and the jumpy marionettes, which were draped in traditional, days-gone-by, West of Ireland garments, diddled and daddled to tunes played on a tin whistle by Hannah while surrounded by circles of bemused Moroccans. Otto, Chawakee and Blueberry took turns at trying to wheedle money from the spectators, smiling while holding out a tambourine, which served well as a begging bowl. Some might say that we weren't treating the children right by asking them to be in on the act, but none of them objected to the request, and when it was over they shared in the gains. I think children are natural show-people anyway for the most part. They may not all like the spotlight, but they nearly all want to take a part, however trivial. Aren't they forever trying to pull the wool over short-sighted parents' eyes, to rosy up those rose-tinted spectacles. They usually learn early that life's a deal easier when Daddy, and especially Mammy think you're happy.

The day's takings weren't great, but when provisions are cheap you don't need a whole lot to make ends meet. Besides, the food there was of a very high quality, much higher than you might find in a supermarket back in Ireland. The vegetables, in particular, were magnificent, all organic, and such a variety. I certainly feasted my eyes, just looking at those pristine potatoes, scarlet carrot clumps, moon-white turnips, onions with spidery roots still clinging to them, fleshy cabbages you could eat raw, dark purply aubergines, police-truncheon courgettes, lotus-like garlic stacked in pyramids and so much more. Fruits were as varied and delicious, and so cheap, except for some more specialised tastes. In particular some exotic varieties of dates and some nuts were costly for most locals, but not of course for well-to-do ones and most tourists.

****

We headed south after stocking up on provisions, hoping to find that des-res site. We had in mind a seaside location near a beach, since, unlike the land beyond its shores which offered few things for free, it offered us many, particularly mussels and cooling bathings, even driftwood for our fires. North towards Taghazoute and beyond was out since it was too built up as far as Taghazoute and too rocky and isolated beyond. Inland towards the High Atlas was also ruled out because the terrain was too inhospitable, too exposed to the sun and devoid of water-sources. So that just left the South, the sparsely populated South.

The road to Tiznit and beyond was, as an added incentive to its exploration, practically devoid of tourists south of the outskirts of Inezgane. My guide book described its attractions, most notably its many excellent beaches and dramatic, bituminous-black, basalt, coastal rocks near to or bordering the main highway.

A signpost for Tifnite pointed invitingly towards the coast, and it seemed as if the road could take us well away from the main road. It was worth a try then, and things looked even better when the paving turned to sand. There was still a track leading on towards a little fishing village in the distance, where barnacle-houses clung tenaciously to petrified, belly-up, beached-whale rocks, so we knew that the area between the paving's end and the village was accessible. It also looked uninhabited and uncultivated so it was likely to have many suitable sites for camping.

Tifnite's rocks cluster round the southern point of a small sickle-shaped cove. The glistening coral grains on the beach are scattered with sea-worn shells, whose inhabitants once ooze-climbed spiral stairways that led to conic and spheric chambers. We settled on a site eventually. Were we settlers then? More like unsettlers, the settled would surely say.

Paddy pitched the tepee at the northern end of the cove, behind the shelter-belt of a sweet-scented eucalyptus grove. The sand-lizards really liked it in there. I can't ever remember seeing so many of them at the same time, rustling fallen spear-leaves as they tried to escape from a searing sun, leaving faintly drawn lines in their wakes as they swam/ran for shelter.

After a couple of restful days spent swimming in the escalator-waved sea and wrenching mussels from outlying rocks at low tide, I began to feel "time" more, to hear its "I haven't gone away. I'm still here", nagging voice. You could say I was bored, but more I think in a things-need-to-be-done-now! than an I-do-wish-something-exciting-would-happen way.

****

I knew that food-stocks were dwindling fast, so I decided to put my frustration-fuelled energy to some use by hitch-hiking to Agadir. There I hoped to acquire some money or foodstuffs by hook or by crook. My voice was my hook, sheathed in pleading phrases targeted to pluck at heartstrings as I approached tourists near the town centre with a hand outstretched in the hope of donations. My crook was, actually, being a crook, stuffing shop-lifted bags of Arabic coffee inside my shirt and trousers in a small supermarket.

Truthfully though, like most impoverished people at the end of their tether, I proved to be a hopelessly incompetent thief. If you want to steal from a shop, the trick is to dress smartly and act confidently (just like they teach you at business school) and above all, to distract a shop-worker's attention by, for instance, asking for some obscure item which, hopefully, will temporarily occupy his/her thoughts while you pocket some choice objects, out-of-mind-out-of-sight.

I was lucky that I wasn't arrested that day, since, even as I was stealing/repossessing the bags of coffee, I had a nagging feeling that I was being watched all the time by the store-man who, without saying a word, followed me to the exit and stared after me as I walked quickly away. Maybe he just didn't want the hassle, maybe he was feeling generous, who knows, but I wasn't going to hang about waiting for an answer.

Later, I boarded a bus bound for Tiznit and, though none of the passengers wanted to buy coffee from me, I managed to get enough for the bus fare in voluntary contributions. As if I hadn't enough to deal with already, nightfall combined with my sense of disorientation and I missed the get-off point for Tifnite.

As soon as I realised that my stop was long gone, I panicked momentarily in silence before resolving to continue on to the walled town of Tiznit. There I hoped to exchange some coffee for a room for the night and something to eat and, as luck would have it, I was approached by a young man as soon as I got off the bus. No doubt he was hoping to do some business with a potentially exploitable tourist. He would have had second thoughts, I'm sure, if he suspected that I was the one who was more likely to do the exploiting. I was, after all, moneyless and able only to offer a couple of bags of purloined coffee as a token to prospective benefactors.

Despite my self professed penury, the local man generously offered to take me to his own house, where he graciously fed and gave me shelter for the night. He accepted the bags of coffee without fuss and, as I sensed that the hospitality tendered would have been given, coffee or no, I thanked him profusely before setting out next morning to hitch-hike back to Tifnite.

I walked out of the walled town, wondering if I should have shut that town gate to keep out marauders. But wasn't I one myself after a fashion, me the infidel interloper? Or could I have been mistaken for a political plotter, the question certainly sprung to mind when a baleful convoy of soldiers in jeeps, lorries and tanks passed me by. Boy did I shudder in my sandals when I saw their suspicious stares, hoping that their fingers weren't feeling itchy.

They were obviously returning from manoeuvres in the Western Sahara and, by the look of them, with their stony gazes and clasped-tight weapons, their minds were still at war. I was more than a bit relieved when I saw them disappear off into the distance. Thinking back I can even imagine how comical it might have looked if they had actually picked me up and given me a lift. I can't help wondering what the reaction might have been back at the camp in Tifnite if I had turned up in a tank full of armed soldiers. I bet that wouldn't have been appreciated. As it happened, soon after a good-Samaritan driver picked me up and drove me as far as the exit for Tifnite.

Chapter 4.

Next day, we struck camp and began the great journey back north to Europe. We bought some provisions at the market in Inezgane and put some fuel in the van before heading out of Agadir along a coastal road bound for Essaouira.

Daylight was fast disappearing as we left Essaouira's outskirts behind. It would have been nice to just park up in the official campsite, but lack of funds meant that we had to look for somewhere for free. Easier said than done you might say, when no signs point the way to a "free" pitch. Where's free anyway anymore, I wonder? Nowhere really, nor anybody, I think.

Squatting was the proper term then for our prospective settling, and "squatters' rights" would protect us. What rights, I ask, in Morocco? Well, the right at least to run away when confronted, claiming dire necessity as your reason for settling where you did; we're all God's creatures after all and entitled to move about freely as long as we respect God's creation. Are we? I know we're not, but arguing the toss sometimes buys time, not too vehemently though as politeness can ease tensions and facilitate timely exits.

Eventually, an explored track led to a eucalyptus wood on the banks of a shallow river. Paddy managed to suspend the tepee cover from an outstretched branch and, after he'd laced up the front overlapping cone edges and tied the cover to pegs driven into the leaf-littered earth, he laid a ground-sheet with a hole cut in it for the hearth on the ground inside. The rest of us brought bedding, food-stuffs, and utensils in from the van. I swear hunger is a more energetic stimulator than adrenalin. The promise of a requital can help you to do things you thought you would never be able to do, to break through that pain barrier into mild hysteria. Laughter the best medicine? You must be joking!

Our settlement setting was both picturesque and tranquil with mature trees filtering sunlight on the banks of a gently flowing, minnow-filled, swallow-swooping river. Once, a wattle-tailed cuckoo perched on a branch right above the tepee's high-collared, open smoke-flaps and sang a sonorous "cuck-coooo, cuck-coooo" phrase before taking to the air again.

A day after pitching camp, Paddy walked into town and met up with a group of English tourists, who were also travelling north and near to broke like us. Paddy persuaded them to come and park up at the eucalyptus wood campsite, having sussed them as harmless yet potentially helpful, hippie-inspired dreamers; "stoned maaan, and don't you just dig the Grateful Dead?" Not really! I'm sure a Grateful Gravedigger would love to dig for them though.

I first became aware of the new arrivals when a bum's rush, literally, sent me running for the "toilet", and by that, particularly in an emergency, I mean anywhere outside the tent and, hopefully not too close by. Of course, when dysentery strikes, as it did for the second time, the "toilet" may easily end up in your pants, but at least I made the effort to transport my soil and stench out of our "living room", not like some in Agadir. They mightn't have been content, I know, to wallow in their own filth, but they sure seemed indifferent, more "natural" some might say.

I'm afraid the "joys" of "Nature" were not permeating my thoughts as I crouched down beside the river and power-hosed the bank with a jet of shit. My aching arse stung like crazy when I shifted sideways with my shorts still round my ankles towards the waters' edge and in. The flow only came up as far as my calves, so it was easy to wash my arse safely, but how safely really when there are millions of tadpoles swimming about, and those you can see. It was best not to think about the microbes you couldn't see. At least the river was away from the town and its shit, which mostly flowed towards the sea without the river's help.

The unfamiliar Bedford campervan barely registered with me when I was rushing by it earlier, but on my way back to my nest I stopped to take a better look. Suddenly, a door swung open and a blonde haired woman stepped out. She asked me if I was looking for someone and, when I told her that I was living in the tepee, she introduced herself and her travelling companions.

"I'm Jan and there's Charly, my husband" she said as she pointed to a man in the driver's seat, "and my children, Ossian, Aurora and Ra are in back".

"Don't forget me!" a voice cautioned from within.

"Indeed, I was just about to mention you Bleep", Jan acknowledged.

Bleep, did you say his name was Bleep, or have you bleeped it out, I felt like saying, but I just said "Hello!" instead. I can't remember his real name, but I'm sure it was Gordon or some such.

I can remember his story however, the one about the prostitute in Corsica who gave him the clap. He was so proud of his venereal accomplishments, so expecting a clap of a different kind altogether. Boy, was he living in a work of fiction, one that was a curious mixture of "Boy's Own" adventures and "Catcher in the rye" yearnings and fumblings. He even wrote about his exploits and once treated us to a reading of a tale with characters who wouldn't have been out of place in a soap opera back home in England. Oooooooh as 'eck as like, they were that borin'.

An agonising toothache, no doubt exacerbated by stress, was about the only thing that distracted me from thinking about my rear. In my frustrated state I tried all I could to kill or at least dull the pain. I chewed cloves, swilled whisky, gargled with cider vinegar, smoked grass of course and would've smoked hash only it was all smoked, and drank some magic mushroom tea.

Now that really did help to numb the pain for a while, but my appetites increased instead of decreasing and my imagination was having a tough time trying to keep up. I realised that I needed what was left of my survival instincts and that other more aesthetic or pantheistic ones had to be left for more settled times. I knew I had to find a dentist and, since I was broke, I knew I could only beg for an immediate extraction. Never "mind the gap"!

Out of the gloom one day Paddy brought us some good news. He'd bought some pharmaceuticals, he said, legal ones at that, that were recommended by a chemist in town. All afflicted gratefully swallowed some of the charcoal-based, belladonna-powered pills. The main ingredient comes from a toxic flowering plant whose name translates as "beautiful woman". How reassuring!

It got its name seemingly because liquid extracts were once squirted into womens' eyes to dilate the pupils. Apparently, the induced "lieveliness", which nowadays might attract suspicious, disproving stares from "law-abiders", was seen as attractive to prospective suitors. Indeed, the plant's other and more common name, Deadly Nightshade was more in tune with how I was feeling. Beautiful ladies, especially with such big eyes, would surely have found my troubles too much.

Beautiful and deadly then, who cared as long as the pills worked, which they seemed to do after a couple of days. At least things didn't get worse and the respite gave the sick some time to recover.

When I felt up to it, I went looking for a dentist in Essaouira. Those massive Portuguese walls didn't make me feel safe, no, they morphed into rows of teeth in my imagination, cud-chewing molars and canine turrets. I had to face the wrecking ball. The writing was on the bleeding wall.

My patchy French proved useful when I saw a promising sign en francais in front of a house on the outskirts of town. The "Dental Practice" advertised might have seemed reassuring to begin with, but as the dentist was an alcoholic Frenchwoman with a dose of the jitters, I ended up feeling more practiced on than perfected. I was grateful though to get rid of the offending tooth and said many "Mercis!" to my slightly stocious Sister of Mercy.

Sore mouth, sore arse, no money, far from home; was this the journey's nadir, maybe, hopefully? No use sitting about though, just waiting for things to improve, feeling like you're losing what little control you imagine you have. Get busy and at least try to steer the ship away from the rocks or look for something that you can hang on to if it founders, I urged myself.

The market in Essaouira was much smaller than the one in Inezgane and, consequently, the pickings from busking were poor indeed. Our marionette show even had a new soundtrack as Jan, Charly and Bleep played Grateful Dead songs on guitars and sang about California. I don't think the dirginess of the music put locals off that much since there's a fair bit of moaning and whining in their own musicmaking. Maybe our puppet show was at fault then. Maybe they thought we were some kind of voodoo circus.

A tourist must have taken pity on us, since she invited some of us up to her hotel room. A giant, six-inch long, green grasshopper looked down at me from on top of the lintel above the door and must have thought I was a taxi because it climbed on to my head. Where to then, I could have asked, but chose instead to stand still while it settled itself.

A long, spindly hind –leg tickled the inside of my left ear, now that was uncomfortable, and those forepaws were clasped tightly round hairs on the top of my head, hairs that were already receding too quickly for my liking. The exotic hairclip did seem to attract some admiring glances, I do remember, but I was that down-at-heel and half-starved that it was in danger of ending up as "Sunday roast".

Hannah was spotted one day drawing water from the river by a local, who reasonably assumed that we were drinking it. He might easily have ignored her, especially as we were obviously foreigners who might even bring trouble, but he tried to make it known to her that the water was unsafe to drink. The only language he needed, seemingly, was sign language, as he lifted a cupped hand up to his lips and then immediately uncupped it and waved his index finger from side to side. He cupped it again and lifted it to his lips, but instead of admonishing, he pointed towards some spot beyond, behind some houses. He was obviously pointing towards a water source, most likely a well used by the locals.

Though we weren't foolhardy enough to drink the river water, Hannah realised that we were on the verge of running out of drinkable water, and there were a whole lot of us to water. She asked me to cross the river and to take a look behind the houses on the other side. A path hemmed in by baked mud walls took me to the wished for well. It all seemed very old world, biblical even, and I couldn't help wondering as I turned the handle to winch up a bucket of water and then filled a plastic container, if one of the local girls would play the part of the marriageable daughter. Some girls were lurking about all right, but they didn't seem interested. Maybe it was just as well, that when I went to the well, I was left well alone. Maybe, like happened to who was it in the bible, I would have been landed with the Whore of Babylon.

Our visits to the well from then on helped, I think, to break down barriers between "us" and "them", and the children of our camp must have pulled at a few heartstrings, because a few days after I found the well a young goatherd who was minding a flock stopped by the tepee and gave some bread and milk to Hannah. He ran off again without looking for anything in return. It was just a generous act. Were we charity cases then? You bet we were!

With barely enough to feed themselves, they still reached out and helped us, strange strangers. What would affluent people do, I wonder, if presented with such neighbours as us drifters? I reckon it's more likely that they'd call the police than feed us.

Poverty can make you do things you normally wouldn't dream of doing, just to make some money. Paddy even invited a couple of local thirty-something men he'd met in town to bring their secret, teenage sweethearts to our campsite. Seemingly, they'd approached Paddy and suggested the idea to him. I'm sure he was reluctant to begin with, especially since there were several strong-minded women in our entourage, but at least he was reasonably fluent in French and could ask them to be discreet and tell them that all had to be obviously consensual.

The secret trysts away from disapproving opinions didn't amount to much after all as the lovers just talked and smooched. I do believe that the girls in particular were rather embarrassed by the whole scenario, and who could blame them? Come to think of it, if tales were told about shenanigans in the gipsy camp, they could hardly have enhanced their reputations.

The pittance raised from the escapade hardly seemed worth the effort afterwards, especially as rumours that were likely to be generated by at least one of the parties, whether boastful ones by a man or "romantic" by an adolescent girl, could only harm our own already threadbare reputations even more.

We were going nowhere fast it seemed, even the objects of pity for the local poor. Didn't European White Folks have the means and machines to help feed Africans, after all, they must have asked? How was it then that we needed to be fed by them? Visions of malnourished Irish children with bloated stomachs made me shudder. Oddly, I felt no such great concern for the children in our campsite. They were still healthy enough for the most part, even those who had contracted dysentery, and still wanted to play.

Sometimes I think that they endured our "crisis" situation better than the adults did. Maybe they sensed that adult authority was all too fallible, but then what else? They surely knew that the locals wouldn't let them starve. Wasn't that enough to be getting along with, enough for the moment anyway. Yes, children live in the now, for the now, much more than adults, but that can be a strength as well as a weakness. Their slates haven't been written on so much, layer upon layer, so they can adapt to accommodate new ideas, even those expressed in different languages, way more easily. Adults, on the other hand, find it hard to adapt. They certainly don't like to be humbled. In truth, they needed much more mollycoddling than the infants, much more reassuring and flattering.

For a fleeting few moments I let my imagination run wild, literally wild. Magic mushrooms had already given me some insights into my wild side, I felt, but how deep was I prepared to delve, I wondered. The brute, the pure animal didn't seem like a state I wanted to visit. Appetites would be more intense of course, and purely of a sensual nature. No need to think too deeply, just eat, drink, sleep, and if you can get it, fuck. That might not seem like such a bad life to some, but then they may have the physical attributes and native cunning that allows them to deter other competitors for territory and mates. I realised that I didn't have either really. I would surely have ended up as a lone wolf, forever on the move and never safe.

The lone wolf must have stirred inside me when I was wondering what to do, where to wander, above all how to get my paws on some money. Casablanca is only a few hours drive from Essauiora on a main road heading north. I was sure that it was worth a visit, especially when my guide book mentioned that there was a British embassy there. Why not Irish, the curious might ask. Because, I tell, there wasn't one. Luckily though, according to my guide book, the British one also dealt with Irish citizens.
****

My achy jaws and shaky muscles helped to spur me on when I decided to set out for Casablanca . They also tried to pin me to the spot however, tearing every which way, demanding to be noticed. My sense of purpose, thankfully, was still there when I needed it badly, needed that push out the door.

I rushed off in a hurry to begin with, but soon when the campsite was out of sight I slowed down and settled into a reluctant amble.

"The buck stops here!", isn't that what the plaque on the US president's desk says? I sure hoped I could make it start in Casablanca, Morocco's White House. I even sang a "you must remember this, a kiss is just a kiss" as I tried to forget that I was broke and had little knowledge of the city. Unpleasant surprises could wait for later, for as late as possible.

I did have Kumal's address, now that at least was somewhere I could go in an emergency, but it would have to be an emergency. I hoped I could get by somehow without turning up like some beggar on his mother's doorstep. Try explaining to someone without the benefit of some common lingo that you met her son on a beach near Agadir and got to know him because you were both living in the same tent.

Mothers may see their sons through rose-tinted glasses, that's true, but wouldn't any one with an ounce of nous have suspected that I was his gay lover. And that was only his mother. Kumal mentioned that his brother was also living there. He was no child either seemingly. Now what would he have to say, I didn't want to know.

My resolve began to dissolve as I waited. My right arm may have been as rigid and extended as a traffic sign to start with, but it soon began to retract, back, back into my imaginary carapace. My itchy arse needed that hand more, it seemed.

Then, of course, a car pulled in in front of me. I pulled the fingers out, and they were a fair way in, and tried to compose myself.

"It's the same old story, a fight for love and glory, a case of do or die. The fundamental things apply as time goes by." sang in my ears, but the only bit of it that made any sense was the "do or die" bit. I'd at least done something. I hoped to live on for another while.

A young Dutch couple in a Renault 4 offered me a lift. They were going all the way, now that cheered me up. Getting stuck out in the sticks was a prospect that I sure didn't look forward to. The relief was short lived however, as I couldn't stop thinking about how I was going to cope, poor homeless foreigner me.

Blend in! Stop looking so desperate! I told myself as I wandered into the old Medina, near the city centre. I was glad to leave those European planned boulevards behind, glad to swap their sharply-angled, wide-open spaces for the Medina's cramped and crammed enclave. There, at least, I didn't look so out of place, so derelict even. I realised almost immediately that I looked sort of prosperous compared to many of the denizens. Indeed I must have seemed only middling poor, me with my shoes that had no holes in them and my fancy red knapsack.

Trudging about aimlessly can be wearying, especially when you have nowhere definite to trudge back to, and it only increases your sense of unease when you can't afford any of the rooms advertised. Rooms indeed, I barely had the price of a cup of cheap coffee and certainly hadn't enough to buy a decent meal.

Eventually, I took the weight off my feet and sat down on a seat outside a small café. I must have looked rather melancholy as I sipped my petit café au lait because another customer asked me if I was lost and in need of guiding. His command of French may have been less than fluent as mine certainly wasn't, but when he realised that I had nowhere to stay for the night, he told me I could sleep in his apartment.

"Any port in a storm!", you might think, is better than none. Of course, it's safer! But what if there are pirates hiding there? It means something else these days anyway. In fact it's quite rude. It's what men who'll fuck anything with the appropriate female genital parts say by way of justification. Men have "ports" too, I know, maybe less welcoming, but "any port in a storm!".

My host didn't seem that way inclined, I have to say, but when he told me he was a barber, I must say it raised suspicions in my mind. The barbershop was conveniently located right next door, so I waited till after he finished work and then followed him back to his place. At least he hadn't tried to hold my hand or make with "googoo" eyes.

As it happened, he was just a generous sort doing a favour for someone less fortunate than himself. His "apartment" was a single room in a tenement, and he even had to share that cell with four others. My sexy fears disappeared when I encountered the throng, which included three militia men and one of their girl-friends. They must have been as puzzled as I was, come to think of it, but they carried on as "normal" anyway. I crawled into in my sleeping bag on the floor and zipped up my shell.

A muezzin's crackly call to prayer issued from a loudspeaker bolted to a nearby minaret as I drifted off into a fitful sleep, and then it was back again, it seemed almost on my next breath.

Dawn's reluctant rays only served to highlight the squalour in the room. I could see steam rising from faces set as death-masks.

"And where's my breakfast?" I joked to myself as I sniffed the putrid, shit-stinking air. I'd had enough of the Kasbah Pauvre and wanted out. Out where though, I wondered as I rolled up my sac a couche. One of the militiamen unfurled a prayer mat and prostrated himself on it as I was leaving.

"Well, at least I know which way is east", I told myself before saying merci and adieu to my Berber barber, not quite bosom, buddy.

I can't remember why I boarded a bus in the city centre later just after dark. Maybe someone told me that its route would take me to Kumal's home on the Rue Vionemale. Maybe I just wanted to sit down somewhere off the streets for a while. It was just my luck then that there was standing room only, or should I say swaying room as the bus driver dashed from quick-stop to quick-stop. He seemed nervous, even paranoid, no doubt with good reason. I looked round at the other passengers and could see no obvious potential troublemakers. Maybe he was just naturally wired up.

I mustn't have seemed that menacing to a young man, who approached me and tried to engage me in conversation.

To begin with, he addressed me in French, but when he found out that I spoke English he invited me out of the blue to come back to his home. Seemingly, he was a student and wanted to practice his English. I immediately accepted the offer. What else could I do? It helped me to buy some time, to delay what seemed the inevitable landing on Kumal's mother's doorstep moment.

His apartment was luxurious, especially when contrasted with my previous night's accommodation, and all his to make use of seemingly because his parents were away for some reason. I'm not sure if his language skills were much improved by our conversations, but I know that I was grateful for the food and shelter he gave me, me who was just some stranger off the street.

The next day I was back on it, wondering as I wandered, "where now?" and later, "why?" as I followed a man I met in the street. "Another kindly stranger, was he?" or maybe one with a sinister intent, I really didn't know either way as I was led away from tourist haunts and out towards the slums that border the cigarette factory. My benefactor/malefactor said I could stay in his home while I was trying to figure out how to get some money, no problem. Always they say there's no problem when there seems to be nothing but problems. It's likely that he thought that mine were exploitable, and who could blame him?

I can't remember if I even cared whether his motives were well intentioned or not as I traipsed along. Then, out of the grey, a familiar brown face interrupted my fatalistic reverie, existential descension, going with the flow, call it what you want. Captain Brahim, the army spy from Tarhazoute, seemed way less surprised to see me than I was to see him. Was he following me, a possible international terrorist, I'm sure I must have suspected at the time? What is the business of military types, after all? The business of suspicion, I'd say, and who is too insignificant to be above it?

Most likely though, the meeting was just a coincidence. Why would Brahim have approached me indeed if he was tailing me? Surely he would have wanted to remain undetected. And why did he tell me not to trust my potential hosts? I believe now he was just looking out for me, but then why didn't he invite me back to his place? Maybe it was some army lodgings, now that would explain that.

I already had a handful, a house full of knaves and jokers before the captain came calling, and his advice, though ace no doubt, should have swayed my decision. Any prudent person would surely have made some excuse and left the iffy locals behind, but I had no money and nowhere to sleep and my judgement was limited by such considerations and by the hunger gnawing at my insides.

I was warier after that all right but still followed the locals, who seemed unperturbed by the Captain's intrusions. Maybe they weren't even aware that Brahim was an army officer since he was dressed in civilian clothes. Possibly they had no idea who he was, just some no account busybody to be ignored in their minds.

Beyond the entrance to the "Casas" cigarettes factory we turned off the main street into a much narrower one. The maze was getting ready to swallow me so it seemed but at least its grid was regular, not convoluted like the Old Medina, which could have you running round in circles while looking for a useful direction. Darkened alleyways beckoned ominously and I was glad that I wasn't led down one off the street which seemed to go on for ever.

Then all of a sudden we were there, stood in front of a shuttered shop front. One of my benefactors unlocked the shutter and rolled it up. He invited me in and when I laid my backpack down he asked me to give it to him. Though there wasn't anything of any appreciable value in it, it was all I had and I'm sure now that I overreacted when asked for it. He pointed up towards an attic space, where he intended to stow the rucksack, a space where I was also meant to occupy, or "coucher" as he said.

Visions of "indebted servitude" came to mind, of a web being spun to stick me fast and suck me dry. My imagination, limited as it was, rebelled at the thought of such possibilities and sounded the alarm.

I grabbed my sack and ran out the door, muttering, no doubt somewhat melodramatically, that "I can't be had for a few breadcrumbs and forever in your debts, thanks very much! Dog eat dog, indeed!"

The hunger even left me for a while as the adrenalin raced, but not for long after I reached the imagined comparative safety of the city centre.

"A sigh is just a sigh", the song from "Casablanca", sang in my mind's ears as I groaned, mocking my sense of desolation. No, it isn't! There's "Aaaaaaah!" and there's "Oooooooh!" and even "Uuuuuuuh!". There's the lightness of bliss and the weight of resignation. My heavy hand reached into a back trouser pocket and drew out a crumpled piece of paper. It had Kumal's mother's address on it.

Luckily, her house was on the same street as a well-known mosque and didn't prove too difficult to find. Plucking up the courage to knock on the door, or was it more like putting up the white flag, wasn't so easy though. I realised that my dishevelled appearance and incomprehensible ramblings could give rise to suspicion and not the sympathy I hoped for, so I tried to make myself more presentable and forced my lips into a grin before knocking meekly.

I grasped the paper scrap with the address on in my other hand, making ready to present it as evidence of my flimsy connection. I doubt if Neville Chamberlain held on more tightly to the one that offered "peace in our time!" . At least mine didn't contain just some fictitious promises, or, I wondered as I waited for the door to swing open, could…?

A figure that wouldn't have seemed out of place on a Christmas card emerged from shadows. "Mother of God!" I almost exhorted, in awe of her impersonation, the cowl, cape and sandals. The colours were quieter though and darker, and of course she was Kumal's mother, not God's.

She accepted my paper scrap nervously and invited me to come in and led me into a living room where I sat down on a wall-hugging sofa. She disappeared then for a while and returned with a young man who looked at me rather suspiciously. Kumal's younger brother made me feel nervous for a while indeed, but not for long. He proved to be helpful in fact as he could speak French well enough and English a little. Maybe his translation and relation of my connection with Kumal were slanted and defamatory or just a version of "told you so!", I can't say, but the establishment of the facts of the nexus seemed to satisfy Kumal's mother.

She graciously laid a tray on the table in front of me and urged me to eat some bread soaked in olive oil and to drink the mint tea. She then lifted her hands up over her face and lowered them immediately while looking straight at me and uttering an open-ended invitation. Kumal's brother explained what she was trying to say, and boy was I glad to accept the offer.

I was a refugee, that's true, seeking refuge from the mean streets of Casablanca, but I know now that I was a privileged one. I had a book in my possession after all that gave me access to and residential rights within the E.E.C. My passport was much more valuable than any bible, or Koran for that matter though Muslims fear to admit it. My little green book could unlock those borders better than Gaddafi's or Mao's little red one and, thankfully wasn't so long winded for such a short story.

"Let him in!" was about the size of it.

Kumal's mother didn't ask for my passport before letting me into her house, nor treat me with suspicion like a border official. She just acted as though it was nothing so strange, as though I, a stranger in off the street, wasn't so unexpected. Her routine was disturbed I'm sure, but she always seemed serene when I saw her, never too quizzical either. She just brought me food on a tray regularly and left me alone to recuperate. I needed that rest and especially the rediscovery of a sense of security, however imaginary.

A television in a corner helped to take my mind off my predicament even more, but its constant trite diet of archaic Arabic orchestral concerts, shoddy soap operas and "News" that rarely ever showed scenes from abroad soon grated. The regular staged entrances of King Hassan in his snow white, caped djellaba, head-to-toe cloak, riding a snow white Arab stallion, were amusing for a while all right, but even the thought of the president of Ireland dressed all in green with a floppy top hat and gold-laced brogues while sat perched on top of a fly agaric mushroom can lose its whimsical appeal in time.

Hassan looked a lot like a KKK Grand Wizard bizarrely, minus the burning cross of course, but I bet some visiting KKK tourists would have felt drawn towards him, and of course repulsed at the same time, being of a superior race and all, all the way from "Alabamy with a banjo on my knee…Hey Hassanah, I mean Susannah, don't you cry for me!"

It was time for me to get on my own horse, to try to grab those fateful reins and steer a course through the chaos, to saddle the metaphorse and kick it into action. My passport declared my provenance and numbered me among the "chosen ones", a choice I intended to exploit to the fullest extent possible. There was no Irish embassy or consulate in Casablanca, so I had to try my luck at the British consulate, which was authorised to deal with Irish citizens on behalf of the Irish government. Sure weren't my father and mother born in the United Kingdom of Great Britain and Ireland, in 1901 and 1913 respectively, I recall reasoning as I prepared to engage with the "Auld enemy". By those criteria I was even entitled to a British passport, well why not!

In the event, since all I was asking for was some assistance in the transfer of funds from a relative in Ireland, I was dealt with politely and promised the assistance. I used their phone to call up my brother Jerry, who promised to send on £100 sterling immediately.

Why didn't I come here earlier, I wondered as I counted out the money which arrived a couple of days later. The woman who paid out smiled condescendingly and warned me, by the way, not to spend it all on hash. As if! I had been prepared to accept a travel ticket along with minimal living expenses like some stranded Germans were offered by their embassy if funds weren't forthcoming, but hoped to get my hands on the cash, cash that my travelling companions down south were badly in need of.

I would have liked to buy some presents for Kumal's mother as a token of my appreciation as well, but there were at least thirteen people in greater need in Essaouira and I also had to buy a bus ticket.

I hurried back to Kumal's mother's place and just stopped for a few moments to thank her before strapping on my rucksack and heading for the Gare Routiere. The bus, though tatty and rickety, felt luxurious to me, certainly a more desirable place to be than those lonely streets outside. Bye bye "hill of beans", I thought as Casablanca gave way to cultivated countryside.

****

The "ones I left behind" were surprised to see me. They thought I was never coming back, mainly because they'd read the postcard I sent them before I went to the British consulate. I didn't know then that I could get my hands on some money easily enough and presumed that they might offer to pay for my transport back to Ireland, or England even. I remember that Paddy was especially grumpy. Mind you he had a right to be since he had fed, sheltered and got me stoned for months for free. I told him that I only planned to head home directly from Casablanca if there was no other reasonable alternative. What use would I have been after all if I went south with just some pittance meant to help me to buy a ticket, maybe just a bus ticket out of

Morocco. Happily, I had enough to buy the fuel we needed for the two campervans to make it as far as Tangier, which was the nearest and cheapest ferry port. Paddy never liked to stay too solemn for long, and a smoke of some weed chilled him out. He blew out some smoke, literally following metaphorically, and pronounced
"what are we waiting for? Let's go!"
The visas on our passports were also on the verge of expiring, so we really had to leave immediately. Otherwise, officials would have had more reasons to bother us, to criminalise us even. In truth though, they would probably only have deported us and left us thanking them for the price of the ferry. Alibabas, we were, not even good for a sneaky bribe.
We struck camp and loaded up the vans in record time, leaving behind a stone-circle fire-place that could puzzle archaeologists in times to come. Naturally, I was in no great hurry, having just returned from my Casablancan odyssey, but I still didn't complain about the abruptness of our departure. How could I when I saw how desperate they were to leave. There's only one way to overcome that feeling of being stuck. You have to move, and now!
My travels through the "maze" may have led me up and then down again, but at least I was finally heading resolutely towards the exit. That exit, in truth, led into another maze, a Spanish "maze", but there it was easier to connect the dots and follow the lines of communication, and ultimately to find your way back home.
Myth has it that Hercules frequented the regions of southern Spain and Morocco in ancient times, where he was variously accused of cattle rustling and orchard slogging. They weren't just any old apples mind, being made of gold and guarded by a fearsome serpent. Doesn't that remind you of another orchard?
Tangier, which is just west of one of Hercules's pillars was, so the story goes, founded by Sophax, who was fathered upon Tingis, who was giant Antaeus's widow, by Hercules. He killed Antaeus, who was a son of Mother Earth, by holding him aloft above the ground, which tended to regenerate his powers on contact, and bear-hugging the breath out of his lungs, sideways presumably since he was so tall, or even upside down.
As odd as myths are, I have to wonder what message this one is trying to tell us. Does it possibly refer to the defeat and conquest of some indigenous Mother Earth worshippers by Herculean sun-worshipping invaders from the east. Coincidentally, Helius reputedly gave Hercules a golden goblet. It was big enough seemingly to use as a boat that was propelled westwards by a lion-skin sail.
The coast road took us through Rabat, present day Capital city of Morocco, and just across the river from Sale, home of the Salle rovers, those famed pirates who kept Daniel Defoe in captivity for a while. We hardly stayed a few moments though, and our only loot was a little green, white and orange teapot, which I bought as a souvenir in the medina. I think I must have rubbed it and wished for a genie to appear. The spout remained silent, mercifully maybe. It could have just been a spectre anyway hiding in there, one portending impending doom.
Islam is the preferred religion in modern day Tangier of course, but where's the logic in the theologic. Islamic calendars are lunar based, so doesn't that mean that the inhabitants worshipped the Earth a long time ago, then the Sun, and now the Moon. I know that's an oversimplification, but how complex is religious affiliation really, and what were the original objects of veneration?
In the first half of the twentieth century Tangier was the administrative centre of a treaty-ratified "International Zone". The local Sultan must have had the most sought after position in Morocco, even more so than the King, though it must have been hard

at times to figure out who was in charge, him or the foreign delegates appointed as his consultants. Back then there was no UN of course, so I'm sure that the delegates were appointed by representatives of superpowers, but what's really changed, I ask, since it's creation? Superpowers still have the powers; and still bicker and horse trade among themselves in their "permanent" Security council. In other words, they use the UN to carry on war by another means.

Who lost most when Moroccan independence in 1956 led to the zone's abolition and Tangier's absorption into the new state? Traders, surely, and their suppliers, but it no longer occupied such a strategic position anyway, what with the increase in Air transport and the shifting of the balance of power towards the USA.

It looked just like any other Moroccan town when our convoy skirted round the old medina and headed straight for the ferry-port a mere 24 years after independence. They were hardly freed, I think. It's more accurate to say that they threw off a foreign yoke and replaced it with an old familiar one.

We managed to scrape enough money, both Moroccan and foreign, together for the tickets we needed and we caught the next ferry back to Spain. How easy it was, really! A few officials glanced at passports and at the contents, human and otherwise, of the vans and waved us through. The Straits of Gibraltar were anything but dire, but then we had our European passports, unlike the many Africans who regularly drown while trying to cross them.

Happily, no great attention was lavished on us by either the Moroccan or Spanish border guards even though we looked gaunt and acted giddy. I'm sure they were experienced enough to realise that smugglers of large quantities of hash like to blend in. We certainly stood out and made no attempt to maintain low profiles. Our "natural highs" were so uncool.

Chapter 5.

After we cleared Spanish customs, the height of our uncoolness culminated in spontaneous celebrations. The champagne corks would have popped if we'd had any champagne, but we didn't need any. All we wanted was to savour the first moments after an escape.

Out of Africa, where we were just another nomadic group among many trying to survive, where there were few state handouts even for citizens and then mostly at the whim of the King, we were reborn as grateful scavengers and squatters. Whatever vestiges of privileged propriety, decorum, knowing one's place, that were there when we went out of Europe and into Africa, were gone, for the time being anyway.

Our castle awaited, the Castellar De La Frontera where we stayed before leaving for Morocco. Fuel supplies were very low, so we had to find a place to set up camp that was remote enough but still not too far away from Algeciras. The castle fitted the bill or, more precisely, a clearing on the side of a bend on the windy road up to it. We scavenged some leftovers at a fruit and vegetable market and raided a skip at a supermarket before heading off to set up camp.

The view was a bella vista, no doubt. Squat pines framed the picture. Rocky outcrops surrounded by scarlet-flowering prickly pear cacti jutted out of a sloping meadow in the foreground where purple-flowering thyme clusters predominated. Beyond, the rugged landscape was softened by palm and pineapple fans, feathery cypresses, crouching low holm oaks, and more, and enlivened by almond blossoms and orangeries. My picture, being a creature of human recollection, may have inaccuracies, mainly of a seasonal type, but its pastiche surely reflects a longing for the ideal. I want the trees to all be flowering, the wild flowers and shrubs to be in bloom, the sun always shining, streams always babbling. Who cares if nature gets played around with a bit? It's always playing with us.

The middle ground was dominated by the Rock of Gibraltar, which looked like a petrified whale emerging from the Mediterranean sea. It was too bad that the frontier was closed at the time, especially since some of our group were UK passport holders and entitled to enter what was and still is British sovereign territory. Charities there could have been tapped, I'm sure, and at least some of us could have begged a way back home to Britain. However, the powers that weren't on speaking terms and we could only cast wistful glances at the Rock of contention.

We were "out of" Africa allright, looking towards it from a mountain-side in Europe, but we soon realised that some very unwelcome creatures had hitched a ride on us. I don't think the lice were trying to switch continents, but they certainly did as they made it "out of" Africa along with us. The head lice were bad enough, not forgotten by most though who'd had them as children, but those body lice, now they were nasty and a new experience for all who cared to admit to an infestation. It's surely a case of evolution in action as different species or subspecies adapt to feed in different environments so all possible arenas are exploited. The head ones stay up there, never moving south of the neck and the body ones stay down below, seeking out hairy, sweaty places like underarms and particularly pubic regions.

My neckline then was their "Tordesillas" line, the dividing line in a continent that was being overrun by two tribes that didn't get on with each other but were prepared to act in concert to colonise my body. What Pope gave them the right, I wonder? I was still weak, not having recovered fully from dysentery, but I wasn't going to go down without a fight, without a "war" on lice, and a chemical one at that.

Paddy bought some industrial strength lice-killer in a chemist shop and all those affected either dosed themselves or, as in the case of the children, were dosed by others. I shaved my head, armpits and pubes before applying the lotion, the better to deprive lice of habitats. I sure looked like I'd come "out" of Africa then. If you'd put a muslim prayer-cap on my bald pate, and examined my tanned, gaunt face, purged lean body and bony limbs, you'd have mistaken me for a Moroccan.

I waited for the lotion to take effect, hoping that the insecticide would kill them all, big and small, and above all, the eggs. It wasn't much use after all if it failed to destroy the yolks, which harboured a new generation. Resurrection at full moon was rumoured as a possibility, so I just had to wait and see, wince I mean because I knew that they like to make their presence felt, morning, noon or night.

******

The wanderlust returned after a few days rest despite my afflictions and I accepted an offer of a lift to Malaga, Picasso's home town. I had some pittance, just a few pesetas it must have been, to help me on my way, a way that seemed awfully long, hungry and exposed to the elements and officials, but I started out anyway, so I thought, on the journey home. Two hirsute Germans in their early twenties invited me to sit in the rear of an old Mercedes Benz, which was pleasant enough in the beginning, nice and roomy particularly after the squashiness of vans, but my ease was soon unnerved by the hairiness of the driving.

Cheech and Chong, German-style, smoked weed and turned up the music, "one step beyond" by Madness, I think, as the driver sped round corners and tried to stay on track. I was relieved when we finally reached flat country and turned on to a motorway, becalmed for a while at least, but then my impatient driver refused to be detained by some massive roadworks. I don't know what he was thinking when he drove onto a rough track that took us on to the opposite carriageway, which was, as any one with eyes could have seen, under construction. Luckily, we escaped official notice, or they may have been too bamboozled to act, as the driver managed to extricate us from the diggings and insert us into the normal flow again.

Cheech and Chong liked soccer, I remember, now that was normal too, but using an orange as a football, kicking it along the floor between aisles in a supermarket we stopped at along the way, hardly was. Once again, we were lucky to escape official intervention. What could they have done, anyway? Wagged their fingers, tut-tutted and sent us on our way?

My initial resolve, or I should say, imaginary resolve, was disappearing fast by the time we reached Malaga, and I decided to abort the mission and return to Castellar, hoping that the return journey would be less nerve-wracking. I can't remember it, so it must have been fairly uneventful.

****

I sure was relieved on my return, knowing I could expect to be fed and sheltered. It's likely I would have ended up alone on some roadside verge instead, grinning uncomfortably at passing drivers while thumbing, trying not to think about the coming night's accommodation. Sleeping rough has its gradations like any other berths, its 5* down to budget/hostel. I appreciated the sleeping space inside Paddy's tepee that night, the warmth and softness of the bedding and particularly the sense of security that being in a group can give. At least I knew I wouldn't wake up next morning covered in dew or worse, or worse still, with some surly face issuing threats in my direction.

Even though my resolve was tested severely and found wanting, I had at least made a go of it, however unprepared. I may not have been ready for road, as the saying goes, but I was prepared to think about it and give myself the time to come up with a plan. I had a cheque for £100 that my brother, Jerry sent to me in Agadir, now that was surely a potentially valuable asset, you might think, but I couldn't cash it anywhere in Morocco or Andalusia. I thought it was about as useful as bogroll at the time, but I'm glad I didn't just throw it away.

Franz, the Mercedes van man, came up with an idea when he heard about my uncashable cheque, one that seemed plausible to me at any rate at the time. He had some train tickets that he'd been given by the German embassy in Rabat, one each for himself, Frieda and their son, that entitled them to travel all the way from Rabat to Hamburg via Madrid and Paris. He gave me the child's ticket, which I rather botched when I tried to change the age of the passenger. A rub of some dirt and a smear of spittle helped to blur the surrounding area, enough I hoped to confuse inspectors. He said I might be able to cash the cheque or facilitate its cashing at the Irish embassy. Then I could send him some money to be collected "Poste restante" at the post office in Algeciras.

****

I'd already had a profitable experience in the consulate in Casablanca, so I was willing to give it a go. I had little alternative anyway and, thankfully, at least the possibility of transport all the way to Madrid and money, and then beyond to Paris. The train was well crowded when I boarded. Now that was good since crowds facilitate covert behaviour. No ticket inspector was on guard on the platform, so I just jumped aboard, nervously fingering a seven year old child's forged ticket while looking for a seat.

Eventually, the train lunged forward and we were on our way. Slowly, it picked up speed and took us away from the sea towards mountains in the interior. I wasn't sorry to leave, but I was a little sad to be completely on my own again. At least I still had a lump of hash to assuage cares and prospects, prospects to dream about as the train slowly moved towards Madrid. I knew I would miss the shebeen-like Bar ONU (United Nations), which was so out of the way that you could only get there by walking along a footpath that led off the road and up through a rocky field. It was always a good place to get a smoke and meet some other drifters. Mind you, the name was hardly appropriate, since the UN in fact doesn't tolerate marijuana use. Bar OIU (United Individuals) would have been a better title, I think.

My nerves were jangled by the sight of so many grim-faced Spanish soldiers. A terrorist/freedom-fighter might have wished for a suicide bomb belt, but then there were the bystanders to consider, most of them Moroccan migrant workers. And since when are those who commit suicide for political reasons so discriminating? Discrimination between peoples is loathsome, I know, but I was prepared to pass myself off as just another Moroccan so the soldiers would be reluctant to engage with me. I brushed past a few in the corridor and peered into a compartment through its opened doorway. I was glad to see Moroccan faces glancing my way, and though they were hardly welcoming, noone objected as I sat down on a bench.

A couple of incidents disturbed the otherwise uneventful journey. Once, after smoking a little pipe of hash, which I shouldn't have, in truth, a soldier who must have opened our door by mistake sniffed the air and glared in my direction while mouthing off some deprecating remarks, no doubt. He was pretty drunk anyway, so his focus was well off, so well off that he banged his head on the doorframe as he was turning to leave. "Ejercito jerkito!", I remember saying to my nodding co-travellers. The other incident also involved a man in a uniform, but as he was a ticket inspector, he was potentially a lot more problematical. Fortunately, he entered the compartment

I was sitting in in the early hours of the morning and barely gave my ticket a second glance as he clipped it. I think he must have thought I was just another Moroccan, and the Arabic script on the ticket may have helped to confuse him. I rested a lot easier after that, knowing that I would make it as far as Madrid at the very least. My uncashable cheque suddenly felt valuable. I fingered it in my pocket. It was itchy with money.

I didn't hang around when the train finally came to a halt in Madrid. I was still a bit nervous, hoping that officious eyes weren't inspecting me as I made a bee-line for the exit (salida). Thankfully, noone in uniform paid me any attention and I walked out of the station unmolested.

Embassies tend to be in affluent areas that are easy to find and spacious compared to cluttered centres and inner city suburbs, so I was able to locate the one I wanted easily enough. There was much humming and hawing over the merits of my cheque, but some telephone enquiries to representatives of the issuers of the cheque seemed to reassure the staff. I was so full of "alegria" when they finally handed over the pesetas, I can tell you, so relieved to be on the lookout for a place to stay for the night. One of the staff told me that Puerto Del Sol, one of those cluttered inner city suburbs, was a good place to find a cheap room for the night, so I decided to go there, not until after I'd strolled around the city centre for a look though.

It was sure nice to have some money again, to be able to afford even the simple luxury of stopping at a café for some coffee. It seemed like a good place to discretely smoke the last of my hash since the seating was on a pavement touching a busy junction. As my smoke drifted and was drawn away by winds and traffic draughts, I could afford another luxury since funds had become available. I could at least think about buying some more. That had to wait though till after I'd found somewhere to stay.

The centre of Madrid fascinated me for a while, especially the statuary and, in particular, a giant, gleaming golden door. I was impressed at the time, I remember, maybe because shiny objects can mesmerise stoned gazes, but if I'd known then what I do now about the possible provenance of the gold I'm sure that I would have been disgusted by its ostentatious display. Maybe it was made from gold that had been paid as ransom for the Incan leader, Atahualpa.

His kidnapper, Pizarro, the conquistadore tyrant, murdered him anyway, despite receiving a fortune in gold, which filled a large room. Was there ever a greater iconoclast, I wonder? Mind you, he probably didn't even think he was destroying so many works of art. To him, most likely, they were just pagan objects that it was his duty to destroy. How fortunate then that they were made of gold, how convenient that all that was needed was a hot enough furnace. Pizarro knew he couldn't lose. As well as helping to defeat the forces of evil, he was facilitating the transformation of the reviled objects into sacred Christian ones. Who could protest if he helped himself to some of the loot as well?

The Metro underground railway conveniently had a stop in Puerta Del Sol. It was way simpler than the Tube in London, which extends tentacles out in every direction and then some more tentacles on some of those tentacles, so I progressed towards my destination with ease. I studied the signs on the buildings near the station and one advertising "pensione" caught my eye. The rooms were cheap, so I just decided to book one for the night and save my weary feet.

I may have been exhausted but after a few hours rest I felt ready for action again. My becalming supply of hash was all smoked, so I was unable to distract my urges and divert my mindset effectively. I took some peseta notes out of my coat pocket and held one up in front of my face. Some Spanish royal stared at me and, to my mind, dared me to exchange him for a puff of smoke.

I went in search in the city centre, where I came across a crusty looking busker, who seemed a likely source of narcotic-related information. I dropped a coin in his begging box and discretely whispered "where is possible buy chocolado?", in rough Spanish of course. The poor fellow was obviously agitated by my enquiry, but I did manage to cajole a name out of him.

The "El Armadillo" bar was only a couple of stops away on the Metro and I approached it hopefully, certainly not with any great trepidation. I could see its sign at the end of a street where nothing seemed noticeably out of the ordinary as I walked towards it. Then, suddenly, a convoy of military and police vehicles appeared out of a side road and parked in front of the pub. Soldiers and police rushed into it and raided it. I could hear a commotion coming from inside, but obviously I no longer wished to enter. I should really have turned round and left the place quickly, but my curiosity got the better of me and I hung around for the show.

Customers were escorted outside and searched at gunpoint by surly "peace-keepers", who looked like they were prepared to go to war. Over what, any sane person could ask? What threat to society could a little bar full of mildly stoned individuals pose anyway? The spectre of Franco still obviously loomed large in Spain at the time, now that could account for the overkill, Franco, that bastion of Christian righteousness along with his friends, Hitler and Mussolini.

One of the assault force eyed me suspiciously and stepped towards me. I was sorry then that I hadn't left the scene earlier, but I had the sense to act the confused tourist and handed him my passport. I tried to convince him that I was just out for a stroll, and my incoherent babble and uncoordinated gestures seemed to throw him. Sensibly, I let on that I hadn't a word of Spanish and he eventually handed me my passport and let me go.

Imagine, I thought afterwards, if I had been in the pub when they raided, if indeed I had bought a lump of hash. I'm sure I would have had plenty time to jettison it, I know, but there sure wouldn't have been any refunds. I had to be grateful for such mercies, but I also had to abort "mission-score smoke". Madrid, I wanted rid of, I'll say, and right away. Who could blame me for wanting to leave it? Adios!

****

I stayed another day just to give myself some time to recuperate and headed for the main railway station on the day after. Funds, which had seemed ample when I first received them, enough possibly even for a train ticket to Paris as well as some smoke, were dwindling fast, so I had to revert to "Boxcar Finbarr", the stowaway train rider. I was hiding in "plain sight" though, trying to pass myself off as a fee-paying passenger.

Fortunately, noone checked my forged ticket on the Spanish side of the border and it was the middle of the night when a French railroad official inspected it on the French side. He may also have been confused by the Arabic script, or just satisfied to receive an authentic seeming document, or just too tired to care, I can only guess, but I was sure glad he didn't hold onto the ticket and gave it back to me.

The Basque country in Northwest France passed by my window unnoticed as the train sped onwards to Paris. It arrivéed at a Gare in the centre around noon and I got out of there as quickly as I dared. The getting away with it rush hit me again as I looked over my shoulder and saw no obvious pursuer. I looked forwards and the Eiffel tower drew me in like a magnet. Jack's magic beans would have found it useful, I thought, as a support, possibly the ultimate climbing-frame. I wonder if Monsieur Eiffel was trying to get at the goose that lays the golden eggs, surely another version of El Dorada, or was he a Babeling God-botherer?

The Arc De Triomphe hardly lived up to its name during the dark days of German occupation. "Hooray, nous avons gagner!", was that what the hordes shouted when it was first unveiled? Later, was it a German version accompanied by a nazi salute? What do they say now? "L'EU gagne!", maybe. The unknown soldier in the tomb beneath the arch had little to cheer about when he was brutally exterminated. Does anyone even know which side he was on?

I didn't cheer, nor shed a tear, when I stopped to look at the epitaph. I was too caught up in my own long march to freedom. Whose side would I have been on anyway in any of the conflicts that have arisen since the erection of the Arch? The politicians, military and "loyal" citizens must surely find it confusing whenever they use it ceremonially. Maybe a name change could help. Try "Arch De Paix" and shrug, don't cheer!

I couldn't help noticing that there were more uniformed people, both police and military, than tourists, everywhere I looked. I thought there had to be some reason, possibly commemorative, and I tentatively asked a policeman "Qu'est ce qui ce passé?"

He eyed me suspiciously and blurted out "hier, le Pape etais ici". Oh, too bad I missed him then, I might have said if I knew the words, but instead I just shrugged and went on my way. The year before, when the Pope had actually visited Ireland and was within easy reach, I had ignored him completely, so if the truth is to be told, it looked like he was following me around, so I didn't need to follow him.

Funds were diminishing fast, so I decided to leave Paris as soon as possible. A traipse around the central sights was about as much tourism as I could afford, and as much as I could be bothered with to be honest. I visited the Louvre, but it was closed, so I never got to be bored by Mona. I would have liked to see the Egyptian stuff though and Gauguin's and VanGogh's. Another time, maybe?

If I'd had the means and inclination of course, I could have ferreted out the haunts of Toulouse L'Autrec and his louche company, or walked by the canal where Van Gogh painted bridges. If I was really obsessive, I might have been drawn towards Pere LaChaise cemetery and Oscar Wilde's or Jim Morisson's grave, or even have tried to pinpoint the spot where Samuel Beckett was stabbed. Is that any weirder than visiting Jesus's execution place, I ask?

****

Roscoff – Cork ferry seemed a good option at the time, I remember, especially since it would have taken me practically to my doorstep, or my mother's doorstep to be more precise. I didn't know what days it sailed on nor how much it cost, but I did know that I had to get on the road again, so I bought a ticket for a train bound for Roscoff, leaving next day.

I stayed in the railway station for the night and slept on the floor in my sleeping bag. It was certainly not a good night's one, but I consoled myself by thinking about that ticket. It was legitimate, now there was a nice change, and there were the views to look forward to, of the suburbs of Paris and the French countryside, especially Brittany. The risk of being stuck somewhere didn't go away, of course, especially since I didn't know if I even had the price of the ferry, but I would be a little closer whatever happened, and I wasn't ashamed to beg a lift. If people don't find it strange to see people hitching lifts from cars and lorries after all, I reasoned, then why should they find it strange to see a person hitching a ride on a ship, or at least on a vehicle boarding it.

The archaeological antiquities of Brittany are many and varied, from the giant, standing out standing stones of Carnac to the intimate cave carvings on the Ile De Gavrinis, but all I saw, unfortunately, were so many streets and fields and little even in the way of wild land. I had an even bigger disappointment waiting for me in Roscoff, however, when I got there. Seemingly, the route to Cork was only operational in the summer.

****

The ferry to Plymouth was though, now there was some hope of advancement, a means to get across the Channel anyway. I had enough money, now there was another plus. Once over there, I knew I would be able to survive a lot easier. There was the language of course, but even more importantly, I had already made use of their welfare system on my way towards Morocco, so I knew how to make a claim.

The Brethren may have left all those years ago, but I was sailing to Plymouth later that evening, wondering about Drake and his piratical exploits and The Mayflower with its puritanical passengers. How different they seem to each other, Drake a foppish epicurean with a licence to take by force while the Plymouth Brethren are portrayed as industrious, modest givers. In reality, Drake's activities didn't have such a bad effect on native Americans, since he was more interested in waylaying Spanish galleons, whereas the Brethren left a lasting legacy, the legacy of settlement and colonisation, and even more strangely, of religious intolerance. Someone should have told them when they were fleeing it back home in England that tolerance shouldn't be confined to Christian sects or even to monotheistic peoples of the bible.

The journey across was short and, though I was glad to arrive, I was even happier to leave dreary Plymouth behind. I hitched to Bristol, where I was glad to be back in some sort of familiar territory, since I'd stayed there for a week just a few months before. I decided not to go back to the squat I'd stayed in then because it had been raided by Drug Squad officers when I was there. In truth, it wasn't hard to find a place to stay despite that, as I met some obliging squatters at the welfare centre

They guided me to an imposing mansion, which was full of people. There wasn't a mad-eyed, stab you in the back junky to be seen, not even a foul-mouthed, cut-up drunk. In fact, the place was well organised, clean and with regular communal meals. No religion or political ideology was forced down my throat. Indeed the food that went down it was delicious, and nutritious, sourced from local fruit and vegetable markets and wholefood shops. The good living helped to rehabilitate me somewhat, and I luxuriated in it while waiting for the much needed government money.

 Once, some TV people turned up at the squat and did some filming. They quizzed some of the squatters and left again, leaving us all puzzled. Later, the results were broadcast on a local news segment on BBC. The commentary was neither damning nor praising, nor even damning with faint praise, so noone was unduly upset. An article in a local newspaper referred to the depiction. I remember looking at the accompanying photo and seeing myself in it. I wondered if my presence had the capacity to bamboozle future social historians.

One fact I can state is that those squatters sheltered and fed me while I was waiting for my handout without once looking to be paid. They didn't even try to cajole me into helping out. I was let go about my business and, thanks to their assistance, I finally got my handout.

I didn't get much, but I treated myself to the luxury of train travel. The ticket to Pembroke nearly broke me all right, but I knew that I would only be one leg away from home. I also knew that I would have to do some begging, but I was sure that the little I needed could be easily procured

In fact, that proved to be the case, and I boarded a ferry bound for Rosslare in the South-East of Ireland just a few hours after arriving in Pembroke.

Part 2.

Winter 1992/93.

Entered Morocco November 13th 1992 and exited on January 27th 1993.

Chapter 1

Twelve years later I returned to Spain on November 8th 1992, having departed from Dublin airport together with my bicycle en route to Malaga airport in Andalusia. I'd bought an old derelict farmhouse in the south-west of Ireland in 1991 and, though it was in need of extensive renovation, I was more than glad to have somewhere I could call my own to come back to on my return, especially since the last time I'd returned from Morocco I'd ended up in my mother's house for a while before moving into a tin-roofed cow shed, where I slept on a mattress laid out on the bare, concrete floor and cooked my food on an iron milk churn adapted as a stove.

Warm air caressed me as I exited the airport terminal building and it was with a light heart that I gratefully swapped the chilly, damp Irish climate for Spanish heat. I mounted my pannier-weighted bicycle and cycled out onto the highway, where I headed towards Algeciras for a few miles before turning right onto a mountain by-road that led past pine-clad hills and roadside stands of tall eucalyptus trees, past small villages with slightly sloped terracotta-tile roofed casas, under circling vultures and above broom-banked, dried-up river channels.

After a few days pedalling, pushing, wine-drinking, olive-scoffing and roadside camping where the highlight was an encounter with a rare spotted owl, who I spotted when searching for somewhere to pitch my tent, I arrived in Ronda. There I marvelled at the view from the old bridge in the town centre into a deep, scrub-daubed gorge where, it is said, people were dumped alive during the Spanish Civil War. This was as far north as I intended to go so I headed out of town on the road leading south to Algeciras. After an hour or so, I pitched my tent in a meadow among flowering Spanish broom bushes, hoping to visit the nearby caves early next morning.

The world renowned Cueva de la Pileta exceeded my expectations thankfully and didn't just turn out to be some dank, gloomy fissure with a smattering of unimpressive stalactites and stalagmites like other caves I've visited. A caretaker/tour guide seemed almost nonchalant as he swung back the iron gate that barred the entrance and ushered me and a middle-aged Dutch couple, who were the only other visitors present, in. He did, however, light the way with a softly glowing hurricane lamp and warned us not to take photos while inside, explaining that the stone-age art was liable to be damaged by excessive lighting.

Inside, I began immediately to see what the fuss was about as I wandered through a natural art gallery. Weird stalagmitic and stalactitic sculptures rose from floors and hung from ceilings and here and there merged to form columns. My imagination saw gothic, looming, calcium castles and spread-winged angels and demons and even organ pipes, which proved to be hollow when tapped by the guide. The ensuing soulful reverberations were, I realised, a link with the stone-age people, who had, no doubt as far as I was concerned, tapped the same pipes 25000 or so years ago during stone-age discos.

Stone-age music still echoed in my ears as I gazed on the stone-age art, which the guide pointed towards while delivering what must have been a spiel that he'd delivered many times before. Still he sounded suitably in awe, and so was I when I recognised the bison and fish and wondered at some mysterious symbols painted on walls at least 25000 years ago, so experts say. The original colours seemed as vivid as ever, now there was a miracle, since they must have come from natural products, perhaps plants or insects.

Nearby a blackened wall showed, so the guide said, where the neolithics once lit fires.

I closed my eyes and tried to imagine a scene from the stone ages, of bodies crouching before rising flames as they waited for fresh-killed meat to cook or grooming each other like a troop of chimpanzees to a backdrop of giant, dancing shadows cast by flickering, fat-fed, oxygen-starved flames on towering walls.
Back on the road again, I passed through a series of "white" towns on my way to Castellar de la Frontera, which I decided to explore further, curious to see if the intervening time since my last visit in 1980 had wrought any noticeable changes.
I walked round the old castle precincts, hoping to meet up with fellow travellers but was disappointed to find only unenthusiastic natives, who made me feel like leaving immediately for Morocco, which lay tantalisingly close by across the Gibraltar Straits. Originally, I'd intended to travel round Andalucia for a couple of months at least, but two weeks into my Spanish sojourn I'd already had enough of the place and I decided to make a break for Africa.
After dark I saw a strange sight in the night sky. A clearly moving light, which didn't seem to be flashing like an airplane light should was, I thought, just some satellite in orbit, but suddenly it emitted a lightning-like flash and shot off into the distance and out of view. UFO, maybe, I conjectured.

Chapter 2.

Within a couple of days I was back in Morocco again, this time though without the protection afforded by an enclosed vehicle, and I sure felt vulnerable as I cycled along from the Spanish enclave of Ceuta into Morocco proper. There I moved slowly through streets peopled with hard-pressed-to-make-ends-meet locals and "wannabe" immigrants, who were lusting after the promised land of Europe as they tried to survive each day as it came in a Limbo, that was more likely to be a waiting-room for purgatory or hell than for any heaven.

An opportunistic man tried to sell me a concrete-block sized brown lump, which he assured me was "very good hash", but I told him that I wasn't interested, though I might have been if the amount proffered was less and more obviously genuine. I reckon it was probably some fake stuff, most likely consisting of compressed henna powder, and where was I going to hide it anyway? Luckily I wasn't accosted by any further "hash" salesmen as paranoia propelled me onwards and I made my way to a campsite further inland, where I set up camp next to an Australian/Serbian couple, who were parked up in a campervan.

The following day, I started to calm down a bit and, as my journey progressed through Tetouan and onto Chefchaouen, I was left alone and only had to beware of dangerous drivers, as one lorry driver in particular almost shunted me off a mountain road, where I was lucky not to end up in a ravine.

Chefchaouen was, and still is, a place of pilgrimage for many Muslims as it lies near the tomb of Moulay Abdessalem Ben Mchich, which is reputed to be one of the four poles of Islam. I was on a pilgrimage of a different kind though, one where there are no shrines to be worshipped at, a pilgrimage of the imagination you might say.

I pitched my tent in a campsite at the edge of town next to dream-machine campervans, whose residents lounged luxuriously or tried to look busy as they purposefully did the chores or prepared for forays into the town centre. The centre was fairly quiet when I visited, and what I remember most was that just-born, blind kitten crawling on the pavement which I almost trod on.

Later, back at the campsite I got talking to some tourists who had passed me by as I was cycling along the road the day before and two of them turned out to be die-hard loyalists from Belfast. Billy and Lizzie were their names and they were travelling with a dreary group of north of Englanders in a sleek dream-machine, seemingly bound eventually for Agadir, just like me. Would I meet them again there?, I wondered, but didn't really care as they were a pair of walking clichés anyway.

As the winding, steeply inclined roads of the interior were taking their toll on my reserves of stamina and, as my life seemed seriously threatened by reckless motorists, I decided to take a bus to the coast and relax for a while by a beach somewhere.

The bus station in Chefchaouen was a chaotic jumble of hawkers, would-be porters eager to wrest luggage from bewildered tourists so they could either escort them to lodgings of their choice or coax some money out of them in exchange for acting as "guides", and on-their-toes travellers, who were mostly gaunt-faced, mountain people with masses of luggage and, sometimes, even goats and chickens in tow.

I knew better than to wait for hordes of "guides" to descend on me, so I chose one at random and asked him to lead me to the bus for Ouezzane, which was due to leave shortly. He hoisted my bike up to a man on the roof who tied it securely and then I boarded safe in the knowledge that it would be accompanying me on the journey.

Ouezzane nestles among hills that once formed part of a border between "governed" and "dissident" territories and is famed for its Zaouia (religious centre), which has attracted hordes of pilgrims since its founding by Moulay Abdallah Es-Shereef in the 1700s. Strange to relate, even though most jews were forced to leave Morocco in fairly recent times, some still make pilgrimages to the tomb of Rabbi Amrane ben Diwane, a Jewish Marabout (saint) who was buried near the town sometime during the 1700s. Did the muslims accept then, I wondered, that the jews may have their own "heaven"? Afterlife apartheid indeed!

I didn't visit either tomb or even look for a Christian one, but I did find a bus which was bound for Kenitra on the coast and I was soon on my way again. The journey took me through some of the most fertile agricultural land in Morocco, past orange groves protected by giant, needle-like, cypress hedges, corn fields irrigated by channelled rivers and stands of dapple-barked eucalyptus trees.

Kenitra is just a few miles from the Atlantic coast and I was anxious to reach the sea before sundown as I hoped to find a suitable campsite for the ensuing night, and I wasn't disappointed when I eventually fetched up at a dune-sheltered site that looked out over a magnificent beach known as "Mehdia Plage". "Surfers' paradise", I thought as I watched the head-high waves lapping the beach. Was there a conveyor-belt hidden beneath the surface, I wondered? They were that regular.

Early next morning, I mounted my bike and set off out of the almost deserted campsite compound for a recreational spin along a road skirting the vast, tide-whispering, soft-focused sky-sea-sand-scape. A sign advertising "reserve biologique" caught my eye and I followed it into a nature reserve, where I cycled along a path that took me through pine-woods that circled a lagoon, where coral-pink, stilt-striding flamingos mingled with variegated flocks of ducks as, above them, thermal-riding marsh-harriers scrutinised the ground below in search of prey and hawks that looked like diminutive kestrels flew from branch to branch through the forest.

After a couple of days spent taking it easy, I was ready to move on again and so I headed back on my bike to Kenitra, where I dodged my way between buses, trucks and overloaded flat-cart-taxis drawn by skeletal nags, past an open-to-the-public-view wall where men stood pissing unselfconsciously, and onto John F Kennedy Avenue in the town centre.

I was more than a bit puzzled to see a thoroughfare in Morocco that was named after an ex-president of the USA, but cold-war politics was, I thought, surely responsible to some degree. After all, King Hassan II did accede to the throne in 1961 around the same time as Kennedy was in power and he must have found it necessary (or expedient) to align his country with either the USA or the USSR. Subsequently, I learned that US troops had been stationed nearby until 1991, when they were sent into action against the Iraqi forces of Saddam Hussein during the Gulf War. Strange bedfellows, etc!

I eventually found the main bus station and boarded a bus bound for the Capital, Rabat, where many years before Daniel Defoe's "Robinson Crusoe" was brought in shackles after being captured by the "Sallee Rover" pirate-navy of the "Republic of Bou Regreg", which was established by Muslim refugees from the former Moorish colony of Andalucia in the seventeenth century.

I headed for the campsite, which I reached by taking a row-boat ferry across the Oued Bou Regreg river to Sale, which is to the north of Rabat itself. The town centre with its modern French-style streetscapes and tree-lined avenues stood out in marked contrast to the surrounding, mediaeval-looking medinas and kasbahs and was dominated by the "Tour Hassan", which is over 150 feet tall and was built at the behest of Yaccoub El Mansour of the Almohad Dynasty in the twelfth century. Close by Mohammed V's earthly remains lay in an onyx tomb on the site of the original Hassan mosque. The true heart of the city though lay, I suspected, in the old kasbah, whose arched gates led into cobble-paved alleys that were flanked by cell-like apartments that crowded in on each other like burrows in a warren.

I was in need of funds, so I had to stay longer than I cared to as I waited for some money, which my brother sent from Ireland to the British embassy. Back again, I thought as I walked into the embassy and asked for assistance, but, at least it was a different city, i.e. Rabat and not Casablanca. Suspicious, they surely were, but they still helped me, though it did take a fortnight for the money to arrive. I'm sure though that my timing didn't help matters since it was around Christmastime.

In the interim I walked the streets or talked to my neighbours at the campsite, swapping travel tales and advice with fellow travellers. A middle-aged Englishman, who had a house in Adare in the west of Ireland and a particular liking for Gambia, said he was waiting for a visa to pass through the troubled territory of Western Sahara on his way overland, while another man from Belgium was likewise waiting on a visa that would allow him to travel off in another direction through Algeria as he cycled towards Libya. I must say that I could understand why the Englishman was willing to brave the desert, where little in the way of human activity was likely to bother him, but I had to ask the Belgian if he was aware of the dangers he could be exposed to, in particular from fundamentalist Islamists, who were waging war in the region.

Besides these individual, independent travellers there were a couple of trucks jam-packed with "Encounter Overland" tourists, who had mostly travelled to Rabat from England and were also waiting for visas to take them through Western Sahara as a prelude to what promised to be a tortuous journey through the whole of Africa as far as Capetown in South Africa. "You'll need more than your fair share of luck to make it to Capetown in that", I said to a couple of Australians who were travelling in an old, seen-better-days Bedford lorry, as he eyed their "magic bus" disapprovingly, and they agreed, adding further that it had already broken down and needed replacement parts even at that early stage of the journey.

The DJ on a companion lorry seemed to have just the one cassette, and boy was I sick of David Bowie after a few nights, well after just a few minutes really. " There you are tumbling in your tin-can, far from old England , exchanging sweat with total strangers, contagion spreading danger…ooowwnnn, Planet Earth is brown and my trousers are still down…"; I paraphrased as I grinned and bore.

Didn't the encounter-overlanders, I wondered, see what they were letting themselves in for when they signed up for their journey, which, I thought, held out prospects that were less likely to compare with the adventures of Indiana Jones, and more likely to involve a mixture of "Lord of the flies" by William Golding, "A happy death" by Albert Camus and "The heart of darkness" by Joseph Conrad.

Almost every day I went to eat at a riverside market, where I dined on fresh fish and a salad of diced onions, tomatoes and peppers steeped in a vinaigrette dressing while looking on at the comings and goings of fisher-boats and row-boat ferries. Quite a few beggars frequented the encroaching area, no doubt hoping to cadge the price of a morsel of food from passers by, and I always tried to make sure I had some coins to offer to some of the outstretched hands of destitute people. They could expect little or no assistance from the state after all and were obliged to beg, borrow or steal in the absence of "gainful" employment, which was unlikely at any rate to be offered to the old, the infirm or to abandoned mothers with babies or young children.

I strolled occasionally through the streets of the old Sale Medina as far as a café looking out onto a square, where I often shared a joint with some locals, trying at the same time to carry on a somewhat limited conversation in French since I couldn't speak Arabic or Berber, even though my French was at best sketchy while the locals' was even sketchier still.

Though I was mostly left unmolested by the locals, one time as I was walking back to the campsite a menacing looking group approached me and one of their number held out a hand cradling a glass phial full of a darkish liquid while at the same time demanding payment for the proffered "hash oil". I tried to explain that I didn't have any money by pointing to my pockets and shaking my head while at the same time slowly edging my way towards a gate that led out of the medina and back to the safety of the campsite.

A couple of days after Christmas day, I finally got the money I'd been waiting for and I as good as ran out of a campsite that was beginning to feel a bit like a prison. I packed up my belongings and cycled to the main bus station where I was hoping to hop a bus for Agadir. Unfortunately, there was an infrequent service and since I was in a hurry to leave, I decided to board a bus bound for Marakech instead. There, my feet hardly touched the ground as I almost immediately boarded another bus bound for Agadir.

I didn't hang around in Agadir for long either because I wanted to get to the campsite on Taghazoute beach as soon as possible, already in my mind's eye picturing myself sitting at a table in a restaurant by the beach chewing on a fish and drinking a cold beer as I let the sun dry me out following a bracing Atlantic swim.

Winter is the busiest season for tourists in Agadir and the surrounding area and I had to do some searching before I found a suitable place to pitch my tent alongside parked up dream-machine or jalopy or somewhere-in-between campervans that were ranged higgledy-piggledy about the campsite compound. Most of my neighbours seemed to be from Germany and I looked forward to being left alone to go about my own business, especially since Germans are renowned for their reserved nature. In fact, it seemed to me as if they were looking right through me at times, even when staring at me, as if I wasn't there, as if my life-force was some technical anomaly which could be filtered out.

Though grateful for their seeming indifference, I didn't always find it easy to ignore them as their yet-to-be-desensitised infants careered about, occasionally stopping to mouth some gibberish at me or to chuck clenched-fistfuls of sand any-which-way. The worst offenders I came across though were a group of young Germans who parked up in a "soooper" dream-machine near my tent the day after my arrival and proceeded to blast out "Knocking on heaven's door" by the "Stone Roses" from the van's sound system, morning, noon and night, day in and day out for what seemed like an eternity. I wasn't the only campsite resident put out by this, but I couldn't just sit by without at least some form of protest as the others seemed prepared to do, and so, early one morning, noticing that the offenders had left a window wide open, I stuck my head through the frame and sang loudly "knock-knock-knock-eeeng on heaven's do-oh-woh-oh-woh" several times before withdrawing my head and going on my way again. There was no response, but some other tourists none too keen on the musical torture being foisted on them tittered their approval and I felt sure that I'd at least brought my disapproval of their lack of consideration for others to the attention of the stone-rosy van-mates.

Chapter 2.

I was well settled in my seaside home when a Mercedes campervan parked up right opposite the entrance to my tent and, wishing to start off on good terms with my new neighbours, I strolled over to the van and asked the occupants if they'd like to drink some mint tea that I'd just brewed on a camp fire. Somewhat taken aback at first, it seemed to me, the two Moroccan (that was a surprise to me) tourists eventually accepted my offer and invited me into the van to take the weight off my legs while we chatted. Noureddine, the driver introduced himself, explaining that he was resident in Germany, where he'd married a local woman who'd given him two children and that he'd returned only for a holiday, which he intended enjoying in company with his friend, Brahim, who was a resident of Casablanca, which was Noureddine's home city.
Seemingly, they planned to visit Taroudant, a walled town in the Souss valley, for a day trip on the morrow and, no doubt encouraged by a few puffs on a joint, which I'd rolled using finger-pinched shavings from a golden-brown lump of hash that I'd bought from a local dealer, Noureddine asked me if I'd like to come along for the ride. Without a moment's hesitation I accepted the offer (after all, it gave me a chance to explore further than the bike could carry me in a day and, besides, I fancied a bit of company and a chance to make use of some native insights and, who knew, I could even make some local connections, which could be useful to me in future) and we all set out early next day for Taroudant.
In the expectation that I would be returning to the camp on the same day, I brought little with me, leaving behind my still pitched tent, my chained-to-an-Argan tree bike and my passport, whose absence would eventually cause problems. How was I to know after all that a week later I'd be in the snow-covered Rif mountains far to the north, having travelled through Marakech and over the Middle Atlas mountains, through the cedar forests round Azrou and, finally to our destination, which was a drug-dealer's mansion near Ketama, the hash capital of North Africa.
The streets of Taroudant were jammed with people trying to sell their goods, mostly trinkets and foodstuffs laid out in front of them on the pavements, and shady alcoves led to shops targeted at tourists, who browsed among display cases containing exotic exhibits such as ancient flintlock muskets, curved daggers with precious-stone-encrusted handles above ornamented sheathes cradling blades driven into the hilt, silver-plated salvers and teapots, lumps of amethyst hewn from the nearby Atlas mountains and much more.
An antiquated musket got me thinking and, as I held it in my hands, I jokingly suggested to my travelling companions that we should start a revolution.
Unsurprisingly, they both shook their heads and ignored my call to arms. Soon after the sun began to set and, as we returned to the van, the pink walls of the town began to merge with the pink glow on the western horizon. Twinkle-flashing stars began to appear in the night sky above towering, spectral palm trees. It was like a picture from the "Arabian nights".
Noureddine sprang a surprise on me, saying that he wanted to travel onwards to the "Cascades d' Ouzoud", which is a renowned beauty-spot named after a spectacular waterfall high in the Middle Atlas mountains and, though reluctant at first, I agreed to accompany them and to share expenses, thinking that we'd be back in Taghazoute in a couple of days. Nothing ventured, as the saying goes. I did have a return ticket for a flight from Malaga on January 4th, but as long as we were able to return to Taghazoute within a few days, I was pretty sure I could make it to Spain on time.

And so we travelled onwards, up over the high mountain pass at Tizi'n'Test, over winding roads with unfenced margins promising certain death to those unlucky enough to stray over them into the precipitous depths below, round the outskirts of palm-fringed Marakech and, finally, down a by-road that led to the cascades.
I could hear the roar of the waterfall as the van pulled into a campsite and there to greet us was a friend of Noureddine's called Yacoub, who immediately went off to make some coffee for his unexpected visitors. I wandered off in the direction of the cascades, past an ancient, cell-like mill-house, where an old woman sat feeding grains of wheat to a crushing mill-stone that was being turned by the force of water, which was flowing through a channel as it sped on towards the waterfall.
A tree-sheltered path led past makeshift stalls selling orange juice and Berber handicrafts, including weighty necklaces with painted metal, egg-shaped baubles strung along with tide-smoothened pieces of rose-pink and sky-blue coral, mini pear-shaped leaves of translucent aquamarine glass and various coloured beads. Even weightier necklaces had several mandarin-orange-sized solid plastic orbs strung together on sturdy threads (seemingly, in pre-plastic times the beads would have been made of amber and would have demonstrated the wearer's wealth to onlookers, particularly those in search of a bride. Nowadays, of course the plastic-ball necklaces are purely decorative and their size only serves to indicate their lack of authenticity.). At least the sparkling rock-crystals strewn on table tops were real.
Some of the stall-holders were a bit stroppy in their approaches to me as I walked along, practically trying to intimidate me into doing business with them, but, as I couldn't afford to lay out any money on luxuries even if I had wanted to, I didn't let the traders detain me as I carried on to the path's end.
And there I finally saw the waterfall in all its glory, thundering over the cliff's edge above into a mist-sprayed cauldron-pool as dare-devil rock-doves flew through rainbows that refracted, reflected and scattered precious sunrays. A troupe of Barbary apes swung precariously above the deep chasm below as they clung to the branches of shrubs that were rooted in the fissures of a cliff-face to the left of the falls. I couldn't have asked for a better show.
That night I slept in a little room at Yacoub's invitation and I rose early next morning, hoping to visit the waterfall before traders or tourists arrived on the scene. The canyon below was still in the shadows and rather cool, but the blood coursing through my veins was warmed by the spectacle. My senses were overwhelmed, save for my taste, which longed for breakfast and drew me back to the campsite, where my nose picked up on the scent of wood-smoke, which was wafting in my direction from an open, darkened doorway.
I cautiously entered an earthen-floored, windowless room, where I found a well-wrapped-up old lady stooping over an iron skillet balanced on rocks enclosing a freshly lit twig fire. On closer inspection I saw that she was baking some pan-bread, no doubt made with flour milled by the nearby mill-stone and, appetite whetted, I indicated to the old woman that I would like some to eat by cupping my right hand and raising it to my lips. Sign language crosses every linguistic boundary and thus it was that I made myself understood to the old woman, who promptly retrieved a round of flat-bread that she'd cooked already from somewhere and handed it to me together with a bowl of midnight-dark, stone-cold-pressed olive-oil dip and a cup of steaming, black coffee poured from a large jug standing by the fire.
The whole scene, with the shawled old woman lit by smoke-suffused rays of light shining through wall-cracks as she tended a twig-crackling fire on the bare earth floor

in the middle of a shadowy cell, the contrasts of light and shade, the timelessness, the softness, all reminded me of a Rembrandt painting, and I was in it.

In the afternoon, accompanied by Yacoub, we visited a nearby hotel/restaurant, which looked out on a lake surrounded by pine-clad, rocky slopes. There, we devoured a tajine-cooked wild boar, which until recently had roamed the forests around, rummaging in nature's larder and menacingly pointing its tusks, beloved of the Moon-Godess, at challengers to its male prowess.

I was under the impression that Noureddine planned to return to Taghazoute within a couple of days, so it was a big surprise to me when he said that he planned to visit a friend in the Rif Mountains at least two days journey further north from the cascades. I protested, but he told me that he wanted to buy some hash from his alleged "friend" and that I was free to make my own way back to Taghazoute. If I'd had my passport on me I could have made the short journey to Malaga without much trouble, but that option wasn't available, so I decided to hang in there, especially since Noureddine said he intended to return to Taghazoute soon after his business was concluded.

I wasn't in such a hurry anyway, plane ticket or not, to return home, and my bike along with my other possessions lay waiting for me down south. I could sell them if I needed the money to finance my return journey or a part of it. Nothing ventured, as the saying goes, once again became my motto.

Back on the road again, we headed north towards Beni Mellal over mountain passes draped with hanging gardens of pin-cushion cacti. We could see the town long before we reached it, stood upon a plateau below the higher reaches of the Middle Atlas range beyond a patchwork-quilt landscape of rectangular fields surrounded by giant, spike-topped cypress fences.

Noureddine knew a café owner there and went with him and myself to a hammam, which is a kind of communal Turkish bath, where the clientele lathered themselves with soap before rinsing with warm water and lay about luxuriating in the soft, steamy atmosphere. I liked the place well enough, but couldn't help feeling somewhat out of place as the only European there, nor did I like to think too much about the possibility of contact with infectious diseases or of the damage wrought on skin by the penetrating moisture.

From there we headed north through cedar-caressed Azrou and on through Fez, where Noureddine drove through the centre of the "new", French-style city that lay cheek-by-jowl alongside ancient walled medinas, medersas, kasbahs and Zaouias. Fez was founded over a millennium ago by Moulay Idriss I and in time became one of the chosen sacred cities of Islam and remains to this day as a living monument to Arabic-Moorish culture.

We soon left the town which gave its name to a type of hat behind and headed towards the Rif Mountains and Ketama. The route took us over a curving landscape past rounded hill-tops quite unlike the jagged-edged Atlas peaks and, finally, we reached our destination, a little sedate-seeming roadside village high up in the mountains.

Too high really, it seemed to me as I was unprepared for the freezing temperatures that are the norm for Rif winters, having left Taghazoute wearing only some light summer clothing in the belief that I was returning there the same day. As I stepped out of the van, a blast of cold Arctic air chilled my already aching bones to the marrow, causing me to shiver as I ran for the shelter of a restaurant. There I sipped a refreshing mint tea while Noureddine and Brahim went off to inquire about Noureddine's friend, who was living nearby.

A local told them how to get there and we headed north for a couple of miles and then looked for signs of the sought-after side-track that led to the desired destination. Many exits to mountain tracks served only to increase Noureddine's confusion and he decided that his best bet was to ask someone on the road for directions. As luck would have it, a van parked up by the side of the road turned out to be occupied by a Bolivian friend of Noureddine's. Who didn't he know, I wondered?

When the Bolivian not just told us the way but also asked if we wanted to snort some coke, Noureddine sure perked up. Brahim was eager too, but I was wary of being asked to buy some so I originally declined the offer before the Bolivian sullenly assured me that the offer had no strings attached. The cocaine warmed me to begin with, sending energetic waves surging through my body, allowing my ice-contracted mind to take in and appreciate the dramatic scenery as Noureddine turned right onto an unpaved track.

We descended steeply, down into a stream-watered valley, past the dilapidated shell of a car (left there to die by an Englishman some time ago, so our host told me later) and into a courtyard, where several expensive vehicles lay parked in front of a two-storey mansion. Immediately on arrival, we were ushered into the living-room by Noureddine's friend, who invited us to sit on a couch under a small, ornately wrought, iron window that offered a view of a distant mountain peak.

He plied us with coffee and showed us some specimens of his home-produced hash, which he hoped to sell us. It then occurred to me that mine host might be under the impression that I was looking to buy a large quantity of hash; hardly a great leap of the imagination for a dealer being visited by a tourist in the middle of remote mountains. On top of that, the numbing effects of the cocaine were wearing off and I could feel the cold reaching in to doubly gain hold of my tensed up nervous system as I examined dark lumps of hash laid out on a table in front of me.

Noureddine rolled a joint and passed it to me, but I was less than impressed with the potency of the enclosed hash. Maybe, I'd thought to himself, it was just as well it wasn't much good. If it was strong, after all, it would only have increased my susceptibility to the cold and would've also certainly increased my paranoia, which could only have been exacerbated by cold shivers as I looked for signs of evil intent in the faces around me while trying too hard not to offend anybody. Besides, it was as well that I didn't have much money, since I might easily have been coerced, in a "friendly" way of course, into buying a load of sub-standard produce.

After all that, our host graciously accepted my excuses, which Noureddine helped to relay in translation, that I was only a tourist with very limited funds, funds that couldn't stretch beyond a couple of ounces at the most. Possibly with an eye to future business prospects, our host then insisted on showing me his harvest, and boy was there lots of it. He led me into a good-sized room that was half filled with unprocessed, harvested cannabis plants, which lay in a heap next to a dozen or so half-hundred-weight see-through plastic bags of compressed black hash before showing me a large mound of peat compost that almost filled another room of a similar size.

Though everything on the outside seemed normal enough, I sensed that mine host and people in general in the hash-fuelled local economic zone were forever on edge, haunted and hunted as they surely were by government forces under increasing pressure, from foreign governments in particular, to clamp down on the hash trade. Guns follow the drug trade where drugs are illegal and, though I only ever saw pistols in the polished leather upholsters of policemen, I'm sure the forces of law and oppressive order had more lethal ones hidden from view. Did I feel safer knowing that they could match the firepower of drug traders? With me in the middle?

If marijuana cultivation was decriminalised where the markets for it exist, I'm sure that the demand for substandard Moroccan hash would soon decrease dramatically. Then the people who live in places like the Rif mountains could earn a living in less stressful ways. Maybe some could even produce high quality hash and restore the good name of "zero zero".

Noureddine hid the two-ounce lump of hash that I bought in the van's upholstery before we set out on the return journey back south, and it was just as well that he did because we were stopped by motorbike cops, resplendent in dark uniforms and sporting polished, leather-holstered pistols dangling from waist belts. Oddly enough, the lack of a passport may have helped me a bit when we were stopped, because I didn't have to engage directly with the policeman. I just nodded and smiled when he looked my way and Noureddine slipped him a 50 dirham note and we were on our way again after a perfunctory search of the van.

If we were travelling north towards the Spanish ferry as opposed to south towards the Atlas mountains I know we would have been far more liable to police scrutiny, so I certainly would advise traffickers to head south first and maybe over to the coast via lesser used roads and then up to Tangier. I myself wouldn't smuggle it in the first place for many reasons. Why put yourself in such danger after all, for a bad product, which you intend to sell to people you don't care about for extortionate prices? Money, is it? Why not just rob them legally by going into "legitimate business"?

Driving conditions on the high mountain passes became treacherous as a snow blizzard turned roads into ice-rinks. A bus slid sideways towards us and just managed to come to a halt before impacting, though it continued to be a hazard to traffic as the fretful driver tried to steer it back to the right side of the road. Noureddine, shaken by the near miss, drove on cautiously, trying to avoid any use of brakes as we travelled through the snow-zone and beyond into the space between the Rif and the Atlas Mountains.

After a couple of days of almost non-stop driving we finally re-entered Marakech, where Noureddine briskly told me that he had no intention of going back to Taghazoute but instead had decided to go to Casablanca, his home town.

Though disconcerted at first to find out that I would have to make my own way back to Taghazoute, I was glad in a way to see the back of Noureddine who, it seemed to me, tended to be overly fastidious at times in his behaviour towards me… "you must eat with this hand…you must wash …you must be polite…etc.

Once Noureddine even upbraided me for not pledging allegiance to the God of my fathers (i.e., the God of the Christians), adding piously that he himself was a follower of Muhammad and his teachings. Brahim, to his credit, was even a bit put off by Noureddine's religious pontifications as he demonstrated when he told Noureddine to, in effect, mind his own business as he reckoned I was entitled to my own beliefs or lack of them as long as I behaved reasonably. At least I think that was the gist of his comments.

Though no tears were shed on parting, I did give Noureddine and Brahim a present of an ounce of hash, or was it I who was given the present of an ounce by Noureddine, our "Dear Leader"? I shoved the lump into a pocket in my mini filofax/wallet and boarded a bus bound for Agadir soon after being dropped off at the bus station. I must have been a bit dozy when I handed the wallet to a policeman who stopped the bus on the way out of Marakech and demanded proof of identity from the grumbling passengers.

It was my only proof of id, I have to say though, and I tried to direct his attention towards the pages that had my name and address and, most importantly, my passport number. To further confuse the issue, I babbled on in English even though I could have answered adequately in French he could have understood, saying "I am a tourist. My passport is in Taghazoute campsite. Here is its number, please". The ruse seemed to work as the policeman took hold of the proffered filofax and gave it a cursory glance before returning it uninspected to me. I breathed a sigh of relief as I saw him turn his attention to other passengers.

When I finally got back to the campsite in Taghazoute, it was with some trepidation that I went in search of my belongings, but I needn't have worried as my tent still stood pitched where I'd left it and all my belongings, including my much-missed passport were still inside and my bike was still chained to an argan tree close by. Now that I'd been reunited with his stuff, I had to consider what my best course of action would be pursuant to, in the first place, immediate survival and, ultimately, towards making my way back home to Ireland.

Chapter 3.

It didn't take a genius to figure out that I could save some money by leaving the campsite and finding a place on the beach, where I could pitch my tent for free, so I immediately went to the campsite office and paid what I owed. I was leaving the safety of an official site behind and taking a risk when I decided to pitch my tent on the beach, but I did manage to gain some company as I set up camp next to another tent and a campervan, which was home to a trio of Englishmen. Our temporary, arbitrary squatters' camp was mutually beneficial and a good example of how things might pan out after the breakdown of official order. Societies may crumble, but other versions will, I think, prevail as people tend to gather together in crises and cooperate. Presuming, of course that fundamentalists won't be running things. Organised religious and political ideologues need the communications network, I'm sure, more than those less committed to causes, and if the networks fail they will lose their edge. Then the more reasonable can gain the day. Until, that is, they rebuild and hand it over to the ones who made the mess to begin with.

The campervan driver/owner invited me in for a cup of tea, no doubt, I thought, in an attempt to suss his new neighbour out and, as we chatted, I looked out of the open back door at bobbing swimmers leaping above wave-crests and occasionally jack-knife-diving into water-walls. Angry shouts suddenly interrupted the calm as a voice with what sounded like an Irish accent penetrated the van; "get out of there, go on, get out of there yeh bastard", it said and, naturally enough, curiosity impelled me to ask "who the hell is that? He sounds Irish if I'm not terribly mistaken. God, something must have really gotten his goat". "No", the now grinning host replied, obviously amused by my comments, " he's actually a German, but he lived in the west of Ireland for many years and still has family there and, it isn't a goat that's bothering him. It's a stray donkey that sometimes wanders onto the beach and shits where he shouldn't and tramples on tents."

A short time after, who should arrive on the scene, only Billy, the die-hard Belfast loyalist I met a month or so earlier in Chefchaouen, who stopped to chat with my teatime companion, not realising that I was in the van as well. Looking much put out by the unexpected re-encounter, all Billy could say when I asked him out of politeness how things were, was "you do know that I kack wath dudder faht"

"I'm going back now to my Brattish compatriots!", he pointedly announced soon afterwards before striding purposefully off. "Jesus!", I said as I looked on, "he could do with a marching band. Was he the one who stole the goat so he could use its skin for a Lambegdrum?".

I knew that I would have to sell my bike soon in order to get my hands on much needed funds, but I promised myself a day-trip in Paradise Valley before I was forced to do so. So, early one morning, I cycled to Banana Village, where I turned left onto a road that led ultimately to the cascades of Imouzzer Des Ida Outanane.

" Paradise Valley! Now there's a name to try and live up to", I thought as I made my way past still shuttered shops and on towards the valley proper, which was overlooked by towering mountains with argan-tree groves clinging to their slopes. Soon I entered the canyon that had been gouged out by aeons of floods and then I began to think "yes, this place is really beautiful" as I looked above at overarching rock-cliffs and below at a clear mountain stream that ran between banks where tall, feather-duster-leaved date-palms grew alongside bushes, whose flowers reminded him of rose-bay willow-herbs.

Once, I stopped and clambered up a leaning date-palm trunk, whose pendant fruits attracted me and I managed to pick a few of its smallish dates, which, gratifyingly, turned out to be sweet and succulent to the taste. The road rose up up up towards the sky, and down below increasingly dramatic vistas of the palm-weaved valley unfolded. I struggled as I pushed my bike up steep inclines, hardly pausing to draw breath until I eventually came to a high plateau, where I recovered as I cycled along between irrigated, cultivated meadows that seemed oddly out of place amidst the wild mountain scenery. Soon I was climbing again as the road took me on towards a sleepy village, where I bought some food and drink from a shop in the marketplace before resuming my journey towards Immouser.

When I finally arrived I felt as exhausted as Sisyphus, but at least knew that my rock had a saddle, adjustable frame, steering and brakes, which meant that it would carry me back home. I parked the bike in a restaurant forecourt and followed the signs that pointed towards the waterfall, which is the main local tourist attraction. My anticipation grew as I walked along a narrow path that skirted a boulder-strewn, gurgling stream and listened out for the blows of crashing waters, but the waterfall merely puffed and I huffed when I saw it. No doubt, the best time to see it was in the aftermath of a rain storm, but noone could doubt the beauty of the setting, the jagged high Atlas ridges surrounding us, the wild scrub and shady trees, the scent of cedar and eucalyptus, and the deep, cool pool disappearing into a cave. I kind of wanted to swim in it but a splash on the face satisfied the urge and I returned to the restaurant and satisfied more pressing urges, hunger and thirst.

Too bad, I thought, when local traders badgered me as I wandered about and fidgety boys seemed intent on relieving me of my bike, too bad that they didn't seem to appreciate the scenery, but who was I to judge them different when I grew up near Blarney, where the locals prefer the sight of dollars to any view they could see from the top of the castle with the stone in it?

The return journey to Taghazoute was almost all downhill, so I freewheeled for most of it and acted the passenger. Lower down, I caught sight of a lakelet veiled in ghost-mist brought on by the encroaching evening's chill. The Lady of the lake came to mind and I kept a mythical eye out for a sword in a laced hand.

Sell up and go! I urged myself on the following day and I commenced the closing down sale. A man in Banana village gave me the equivalent of £60 for the bike, which I'd bought secondhand for £100, now that was a good start, and I got the equivalent of £20 for an unused pair of German-made leather shoes from a man in Taghazoute. I gave some bits and pieces, including a large plastic sheet that acted as a protective barrier for my tent, away to my squatter friends and so further lightened my ever dwindling load and left Taghazoute behind.

I bussed it north from Agadir along the coast as far as Ceuta, where I boarded a ferry bound for Algeciras in Spain. Though initially relieved to be back in Spain again, I didn't have much time or means to celebrate my good fortune. In fact I was almost stony broke and was forced to sleep in the town square that same night. I looked over at the Rock of Gibraltar next morning and hoped it could be the "rock" I could lean on. Algecirans seemed a rather unfriendly lot, and I was just another penniless tourist to be looked down upon to them, I'd say, and a probably less deserving one than some desperate Africans, who may have walked half a continent to get there, but I did have the option to give the Rock a go, which they certainly hadn't.

Fortunately, unlike the previous time I was in Algeciras a dozen years before, the frontier with Gibraltar was open to people travelling from Spain, so I made my way through the town of La Linea and on towards the border, all the while trying to reassure myself that I had no need to be afraid of being confronted by gun-toting, shoot-first-ask-questions-later, SAS-trained, British soldiers. My paranoia, though somewhat overreactive, had some basis in reality, I can plead, because recently an SAS hit-squad had shot dead three Irish members of a so-called, "terrorist" cell, who were trying to cross the very same border I was now approaching nervously.

As it turned out, I had no problem whatsoever at the border, where the unconcerned officials waved me through after briefly checking my passport. Bizarrely, I then had to wait at a set of traffic lights which controlled traffic traversing the isthmus between Spain and the Rock until a plane had taken off from a runway that spanned the entire width of the narrow neck of land. A bright red London double decker bus took me in to the centre of a lively town, which boasted an eclectic mixture of old-style British-colonial architecture and modern highish-rise buildings that were mostly occupied by banks and other financial institutions drawn to set up there by attractive financial inducements.

I noticed that the iffy BCCI bank had an expensive looking building there. "Who knows how much dodgy money is keeping the Gibraltar economy afloat", I'd thought as I strolled along main-street, past a statuesque guardsman stood outside a government building and on past a small group of Moroccan immigrant workers, who were holding up placards that pleaded for better treatment for them and their fellow-countrymen. I could empathise for a few moments, but my own needs were soon uppermost in my mind, needs that were not going to be satisfied by any of the dodgy money dealers.

I looked round for clues, especially for what could pass for rough livers, and plucked up the courage to ask some likely prospects where I could find something to eat. They were French, I soon found out, and I made my pitch as best I could, but "faim" and "pas de chambre et d'argent" were all the French I needed. Noone said "Allez mendicant!", as it happened and a man offered to take me to a Protestant-run soup-kitchen, where I ate ravenously.

Afterwards, he brought me to a backstreet squat, which could only be entered through an open window since the door leading onto the street was barricaded against intruders. Their's was quite the alternative "soap opera" and I was just another fleeting guest careering their direction from out of who knew where. I blew in and out again after a couple of days as the wings of Fortune flew my way. A fellow squatter told me that a local catholic priest might be willing to help me get a flight to London, whether or not I could pay for it.

I did have a cheque for £100 sterling made out in my name which was sent to me by my brother, which I couldn't cash there or in Spain no matter how much I tried, but it gave me some confidence when I went in search of my potential benefactor. He heard me out patiently when I got to talk to him in his office, and though he looked suspicious when I gave him the cheque, I pointed out that my name was on it and showed him my passport and told him to make a note of the number. I also showed him the unused return ticket for Malaga airport and said I' been unavoidably detained in Morocco.

I'm not sure I needed to put on such a show, but I didn't have much else to think about at the time. Either way, I got the "golden" ticket, which was provided by a travel agent who was contacted by the priest.

The runway at Gibraltar airport must be one of the shortest anywhere in the world and, though I felt a fearful adrenalin rush as the plane taxied briefly to one end of it and was then launched hell-for-leather at the other end, my mood was light as I, whew just made, said goodbye to Gibraltar.

London was freezing when I got there, and I was sure glad I had safer options to exploit than those open to me in Gibraltar. I stayed with some friends in Clapton in the East End and signed on the dole immediately. A few days later I got the cheque and headed straight for the Irish Centre in Camden Town, where I asked for some assistance to get back to Ireland. The social worker who dealt with me told me I would be better off staying at home in future after she'd booked a ticket for me on a ferry. If only she knew where I'd been.

Part 3.

Summer 1994

Chapter 1.

I left Dublin airport on June 6th 1994 on a plane bound for Agadir in the south of Morocco. I was glad to be able to go straight to my desired destination unlike previous visits which involved either travelling overland all the way from Ireland or making my way from southern Spain through the north of Morocco and down to the southern coast.

The sun was splitting the stones as I got off the plane and I immediately went in search of a cheap hotel, where I could stow my luggage before going off to get something to eat. I checked out of the hotel early next morning and boarded a bus bound for my favourite beach at Taghazoute, where I planned to stay in a tent at the campsite. My spirits were lifted by a combination of lively, melodious, modern Arabic music emanating from the crackly bus sound system and the sights passing by, especially the bustling fishing port and the thorny mountain slopes that stretched off into the sun-bedazzled distance. The camping gas plant still made me shudder though as its explosive potential was huge, and who could predict when the next earthquake might sever the pipes and carve a new beach out of the rocky land between it and the nearby ocean?

The campsite was quiet enough so I had no trouble finding a place to pitch my tent. Winter is normally the busiest time for tourists in the area as mostly northern or western Europeans make their way south to avoid their own cold, damp climates. Native tourists were a lot more common, no doubt drawn away from the baking interior by the less intense temperatures of the coast and, of course, by the desire to bathe in the cooling sea.

Highs besides those of the sea were constantly in my mind as I went in search of a smoke, and I soon found a dealer in one of the makeshift restaurants on the path leading to the beach. I think he deserves an alias, so I'll call him Said, not just because of his trade, but also his inability to keep his temper, or word. He said he'd call round to my tent within a couple of hours, now that he did, and most importantly, he had a nice sized lump of golden-brown hash. I gave him what he asked for, knowing that I was getting a bargain by Irish standards and then rolled a spliff.

Said must have sensed that I was ripe for further exploitation as he told me that his parents had an empty room in the village if I was interested. It wasn't a whole lot dearer than my back-stiffening tent so I told him I'd have a look at it on the following day. Though barely furnished, with just a timber frame to sleep on, it had a soothing view of the strand and sea framed by a square, glassless window-frame. I strung my Brazilian-bought hammock from pegs attached to the walls and lay in it while gazing out the window and felt right at home. I mightn't have been so quick to part with a week's rent up front if I could have predicted the immediate future, but who can with certainty? Maybe, given the apparently hyperish nature of Said, I should have said No when he asked me if I had any alcohol.

Too polite I was, thinking I might simply drink a toast in honour of my new residence in company with my landlord. I rummaged in my luggage and fished out a large bottle of rum and poured a little into two plastic tumblers and topped them up with liberal amounts of coca-cola before handing one to Said.

All seemed well, but one sip soon changed things for the worse. A second drained the cup and he then grabbed a hold of the bottle and took an almighty swig of neat rum. His speech began to sound more and more incoherent as he tried to explain that he needed to go and see someone and, at that stage, I was only too glad to see him go. If I'd known he was going to come back for some more, I might have disposed of the bottle or gone out for a while, but I'd paid for the room, and the bottle as well to be fair, so I might not.

He had a pal in tow, now that seemed more sociable, and a ghetto-blaster, so I assumed that we were going to have a party of sorts. However, I believe Said just wanted to go straight to the passing out bit. Well, at least he didn't mistake me for an object he wished to dance with mercifully. Oh no, that privilege was reserved for the bottle of rum which he drank deeply from before passing it to his pal, who, if the truth be told, seemed a pleasant enough chap and only took a little sip before handing it back again to Said.

I didn't like the music either, but did he really need to hurl the ghetto-blaster against the wall? Would you blame me for not seeing the funny side to such tantrums and for looking for a quick exit? Fundamentalism wasn't such an issue back then, I know, so at least I wasn't threatened with a beheading. Said would definitely have adopted such attitudes if it was, I'm sure. But would they adopt such as him in the 2000s? Maybe as a potential suicide bomber, I'd say. In fact I found out later that he was universally disliked, but, of course, there was something else to exploit for Islamists.

My back was against the wall for real as I edged past Said and ran out the door. I stopped and turned round to see if he was coming after me, but, to my relief, only his pal emerged. He apologised without any prompt for Said's antics and offered to take me immediately to see Said's parents, who were very helpful. Said's father went back to the scene of the disturbance with me and offered me the use of another room of his nearby for the coming night when he saw the state his son was in.

Said's father distracted his son while I gathered up my belongings, but where was the hash? I panicked a bit when I realised I didn't have it. And then, phew, there it was on the outstretched palm of Said's father, who picked it up off the floor. I wouldn't say he was smiling, but I'm sure he was a bit less anxious knowing that it was highly unlikely that I would involve the police. And he was right.

What use would that have done me anyway? I might have been delayed and asked to testify who knew when, and for what return? I had the key as well and Said's father told me to come back next day when Said had left and move back in. After all I'd paid Said for a whole week up front and, as far as I was concerned, I was entitled to what I'd paid for.

When I did return early next morning I wasn't sure what to expect as I pushed in the slightly ajar door, but, Bismillah, as they say locally, he'd fled the scene. With that, I decided to make myself at home as I bolted the door against any further unwelcome interruptions. Said did return a couple of times during the week, but I never left him in and told him to go away. He was just another village idiot to be fair, and I've met my fair share of those in the pubs of Kiskeam and Newmarket in north Cork

Aside from Said's intrusions, I spent a pleasant week in the village, swimming everyday in the sea and cooking meals for myself in a little clay tajine and saucepan heated by a little portable gas ring. I'd bought the cooking implements in the village to fry up some fresh vegetables and, occasionally, a couple of glistening, ochre-yoked eggs in some jet-black olive oil and to boil some potatoes or rice and water for refreshing mint tea drinks.

After a week I was ready for road and thinking about modes of transport. Mopeds were everywhere I looked, so I reckoned I would be able to pick one up second-hand cheap enough. My enquiries led me to a motorcycle shop in Inezgane, where I bought a Peugeot Cent-trois of an indeterminate age for about 300 pounds. It seemed a bit expensive, but I reassured myself that I would be able to recoup a large amount of the cost when I, hopefully, would resell it before returning to Ireland.

I moved back into my tent at the campsite when I left the claustrophobic village behind and soon began to appreciate the "open" again as I smoked a spliff and lay in my hammock, which dangled from low growing, argan trees, and planned ahead. The moped had carried me along the flat coastal plain from Inezgane to Taghazoute without any bother, but I wondered how it would cope with steep mountain roads. A drive in Paradise valley would test it, I decided, and headed off in that direction soon after setting up camp.

Two years before I had to expend some effort as I cycled along the same road, but the moped took the effort out of the trip and I could take in the idyllic views at my ease, caressed by a bow-wave breeze as I zipped along through an oasis-valley canyon towards the steep inclines that led on to Immouzer des Ida Outanane.

At the beginning of the sharp ascent the moped trundled along comfortably enough in a low gear. I looked back at the exhaust and the smoke was no blacker, so the engine wasn't obviously knackered, I guessed. As the road grew progressively steeper, the moped was finding it more and more difficult to carry my weight and soon it came to an exasperating halt. I had to get off and push, but was compensated by the fact that I only had to steer as the engine easily impelled the lightened moped up the steeply inclined road and onto a plateau. It lacked power, I knew, but was going well enough.

I remounted and drove between irrigated meadows that lay beneath towering sentinel date-palms, stopping briefly to drink an orange juice at a roadside café before taking to the road again, on towards the end of the plateau and up as far as a mountain village. Though I wasn't far from the waterfall I'd visited two years before on a push- bike, I decided to return to the campsite, happy enough in the knowledge that the moped wasn't a complete crock and, hopeful, at least, that it would be able to carry me for a substantial part of my upcoming voyage of discovery.

I felt a sense of freedom as I exited the campsite, all-packed-up and ready-for-road and resplendent in t-shirt, shorts, plastic sandals and baseball-cap helmet. I blended in with other natives on the move, which was my wish and soon began to have their disregard for traffic regulations, not to a reckless extent though, unlike some. I planned to travel over the Anti Atlas mountains as far as the outskirts of the Sahara desert, then back north on a loop to Marakech by way of the cedar forests of Azrou and the Cascades d' Ouzoud.

I drove through the Souss valley as far as Taroudant and beyond, past the turn off for the high mountain pass of Tizi'n'Test, which leads onto Marakech, and on past the Anti-Atlas mountain range of Djebel Sirwa to Taliouine in a couple of days. At least I drove most of the way because I got a puncture some distance from Talouine after I left the roadside hotel I stayed in on my first night on the road and a local man took me along with my moped in his van all the way to Talouine. He didn't mention money either or look business-like, but did put a bit of business the way of a bicycle repair shop, which he pointed me towards and a man fixed my puncture for a few dirhams. It was getting dark, so I decided to stay in town for the night in a large, almost empty hotel, right up on the fourth floor. It seemed very European until I looked out the window at the arches in the town square below and the desolate mountain landscape beyond.

Early next morning, I headed east again, on towards Tazenakht and then north towards the intersection with the road from Marakech to Ouarzazate. I turned south east towards Ouarzazate, where I booked into a town centre hotel. There I rested and contemplated my next moves, unaware of the twist fate had in store for me. Ouarzazate is at the centre of a thriving film-making industry that attracts film companies from afar with a combination of top-of-the-range indoor and outdoor facilities, great locations and inexpensive extras, mostly garnered from the local population. I, by happenstance, would soon become part of it, albeit just as an extra.

Chapter 2.

The producer of a film based on a biblical affair between King Solomon and the queen of Sheba was on the lookout for extras of a more western appearance, probably to widen the film's appeal to white evangelist Americans in particular. I was approached by a local man who was working for the film company and was prepared to give it a go. In truth, I never thought I'd be hired for my looks, and for a bogus reason at that, because the film was meant to be about the affair between King Solomon and the Queen of Sheba and should thus, if historical authenticity was the yardstick for choosing racial stereotypes, have sent scouts out looking for Middle-Eastern look-alikes. It was fiction though, I justified, and sure to be someway entertaining, and it paid about £150 a week.

What was I going to be, I asked? and must have looked astounded when the "talent" scout said "a member of Solomon's cavalry". "But I only ever rode horses a couple of times", I explained, and he just said that some of the other extras hadn't even ridden one once. How the French instructor must have wished for a Mongol horde when he greeted us early next morning! However, he undoubtedly knew what he could expect as he shrugged a few Gallic shrugs and resignedly led the "cavalry" past the film studio hangar into a corral, where about a dozen scrawny, less-than-eager-to-please horses awaited their and our humiliations.

Some foolhardy youths made a beeline for the friskiest nags they could find, and who was I to upstage them, I by the way pretended to myself as I asked the instructor in halting French to find me a quiet mount. In fact, I wasn't sure if it had been stuffed as well as mounted when I climbed on its back, it was that immobile. I did manage to prod it into action eventually and it trudged round the studio lot. Why the long face?, I whispered in a floppy ear, but it didn't get the joke.

I did stay in the saddle though, unlike one "knight", who was thrown violently by his mount and badly bruised. I'd say he probably knew nothing about horses until the incident, and that his first lesson was hard learned. Learn how to fall before you learn how not to, applies in so many situations. I was glad to fall off my saddle ay the end of the drill, deliberately, as I dismounted awkwardly. It hardly deserved the description, I thought, as it was really just a threadbare blanket tied on with a less than secure belt, and those stirrups would have made good budgie roosts but my feet kept rolling forward on them.

I was definitely not at my most presentable when I posed to be photographed as a prelude to signing a contract, which guaranteed me a week's wages at the very least, even if I was unable for some reason to complete a whole week. Arthritic, due in large part to my saddle sore backside, and unkempt, with hair askew and sand in my eyes, up my nose and all over the rest of me, fitted my description. I suppose I was some bit closer to portraying the reality of a cavalryman's condition in Solomon's army. Not much though!

I happily exchanged four legs for four wheels as I boarded a bus bound for the town centre and rested up in my room in the Hotel Royal. I looked forward, though my posterior might not have, to the morrow, when I was due to be driven to a nearby oasis.

A truck picked me up along with some other extras early next morning and took us north along the main road for a few miles and then veered left onto a winding desert track. The oasis appeared as if out of a mirage down below in a valley, which was originally hidden from view. Horses tied to ancient, stocky date palms lingered on the shadier sides and stooped to nuzzle foodstuffs as people scurried between large marquee tents. One was a fitting room for costumiers and another was the dining room, where tables were laden down with piled-high plates.

It was off bounds to us extras though, an "overseer" let me know when I tried to help myself to some of the feast. Were they trying to "classify" us then, I wondered, to help us get in the mood for playing the minions of a flaky despot, who had the power of life and death over us?

Our sandwiches would be delivered to us outside, where we were meant to wait alongside our horses, thank you and be grateful!

I left the guardian of the cornucopia behind and went off in search of the nag I'd been riding the day before, grumbling to myself. Heigh-Ho Silver barely acknowledged my presence as she shuffled, lattice-dappled by sunlight filtering through overhanging palm branches. "Up and away!", indeed, I mocked us both, thinking "Go away!" was on those jowly lips. When my sandwich came, I chewed it just like another beast of burden and waited for further instructions.

Soon I was sent to the wardrobe tent where I was decked out in pseudo-biblical fashion. Fumbly hands wrapped a piece of cloth around my waist and between my legs like an adult nappy, which was complemented by a shaggy "hair shirt" vest. If Saint Francis had to wear the like, I thought, I didn't envy him, nor the poor sods who might have worn flimsy, laced-up, leather sandals the like of which I was shod with. To complete the "terrifying" effect, a firmly wound turban looked more like a little old lady's fancy hat and my mocky-up sword wouldn't have sliced bread.

Waiting then, then some more waiting, then finally my cavalry-mates and I were asked to mount up and follow King Solomon, who was played by the Hollywood actor, Jimmy Smits. I didn't for a moment believe that Solomon's cavalry was composed of upright, moral, "goodly" knights in reality, so I leered menacingly as we rode past a strategically positioned camera and urged "Come on Solomon! Lead us to battle! My sword is thirsty for blood. My manhood aches for virgins. My stash needs replenishing with gold and precious stones".

No doubt, the film's American evangelist financier would have been appalled by my interpretation of the role of one of Solomon's cavalry-guard as a blood-thirsty barbarian, but then his own interpretation was surely self-serving and even more of a lie than one my fantasising could conjure up.

Solomon's cavalry was most probably, after all, a ragtag of mercenaries, who joined up for the rape and pillage and soldiers captured in battle, who were given a choice between immediate execution and, most probably, a subsequent glorious death in battle. The few who actually wished to lay down their lives for the king were, paradoxically, probably the biggest cowards, because they were, most likely, more afraid of the king than the others. They could still slaughter an innocent child if ordered to do so, mind you, the "brave" upholders of tradition.

After a break for lunch, the scene switched to a nearby watering hole, where cameras were set up to record a meeting between Solomon and the Queen of Sheba. Us cavalry cantered after Solomon, who steered his horse into the pond and headed straight for Sheba on the opposite bank, splash-splashing as he treaded water before abruptly reining in just in front of the awe-struck, yet strangely demure, Queen, who was played by Halle Berry. I was a knight then in the game of chess, I guessed as I managed to persuade Silver to keep up with the pace. Trouble was I found it hard to slow her down as she waded into the pond and she moved like a knight, that is a couple of paces one way and then one off to the side and almost stumbled into the Queen of Sheba. Some might say that I was a scene stealer, a knave who wanted to upstage the King and Queen.

On the following day, the scene switched again as cameras were set up on a ridge overlooking a shallow, rugged canyon, where Solomon and his cavalry were to be subjected to an ambush by hostile forces. We had to wait out of sight in a sandy valley behind the ridge where the cameras were pointing the other way while equipment was being tested and camera angles adjusted. It was baking hot, enough to scramble your brains, and the unedifying spectacle of horny stallions exhibiting their erect members could hardly have passed for entertainment. Beyond the hill though was a battle scene in the making and I

longed to see the spectacle, so longed that I, against orders, climbed on up accompanied by another extra, who was a Moroccan school teacher with some English.
All might have gone by unnoticed if we hadn't strayed into shot as we made our way towards the cameras that were trained on King Solomon, who was under attack from a barrage of untipped arrows shot into the air from spring-loaded machines. It was only when the King got up off the ground again after his horse stumbled and he fell off that I noticed he wasn't Smits but was in fact the French riding instructor. He'd obviously faked the fall and in the next take here lies Smits as Solomon.
We could have passed for skulkers, dressed as we were for the parts, I should have told Antonio Gabrelli, the diminutive Italian producer, but there was no reasoning with the intemperate tyrant. He rushed over to us and told us to leave at once. Of course we assumed that he was ordering us to rejoin the other extras in the valley below, but when I apologised and asked if that was his intention, he said "No, you're both fired! Now go!"
"What's the big deal? Do you think we were trying deliberately to sabotage the filming? Haven't you ever screwed up a scene yourself?", I complained before trying to limit the damage to myself. I explained that I'd taken the job because I was asked to by someone working for the same company as him and did so out of curiosity mostly and not necessity like the school teacher, but the bastard still wouldn't even reinstate him.
Flabbergasted, bemused, annoyed, I couldn't think what to do next, so I gave vent to my rage by chucking my turban at the object of my loathing before marching off in the direction of the wardrobe tent. I calmed down soon enough though when someone told me that I'd still get my week's wages despite being sacked after a couple of days. Gossip had it that Signor Caligula had a reputation for firing people left, right and centre, even that his antics were about the only truly dramatic scenes to be seen.
In truth, as it happened, I'd done well out of the deal as I'd had enough of waiting round in the searing heat, seen enough of the art of film-making as it happens and been bored enough by the insipid snippets of overheard on-screen dialogue. Solomon and the Queen of Sheba indeed! It was more like something from Mills and Boon.
I walked out of the pages of the Bible, knowing that I'd be getting compensated for the ordeal. Now there was a turn up for the "good" book, whose effects I'd ever before endured without reward. A van stopped for me as I strolled along the track back home and dropped me off outside my hotel, where my room seemed like a restful sanctuary after the battles of the day.
I was a free man again and back to being a tourist, so I went to visit a local landmark on the following day called the Kasbah Taorirt, where crumbling, fading-sunset-coloured walls enclosed shadowy, arched corridors that serviced a warren of darkened room-burrows within a fort. A tiny little girl looked up at me as I strolled along a corridor, and I couldn't figure out how her eyes were so bright, even in the shade. A tout approached and I was brought down to Earth again as the young man tried to drum up some business. I must have been feeling a bit flush, with the wages to come in mind, because I said I'd have a look. His was a small family concern, which appealed to me more than some big company might have, and was just a few paces away up a small flight of steps.
Inside, the tout introduced his future father-in-law and his betrothed bride-to-be, who were busily engaged in stringing necklaces together in a space cluttered with display cases full of jewellery and piles of Atlas-Mountain-weaved carpets. Betrothed indeed, I thought, and how many carpets and trinkets will he get as a dowry? I must admit that I could have felt jealous, but what was the cost to him? All that fawning and pretence until the wedding, and then what? Well he found out eventually.
I bought some trinkets, which had to satisfy me in lieu of a bride to be, and made my exit. Beyond the mediaeval fort I could see wicker fences that were trying in vain to hold back the

inundations of the desert-sea, whose still-life sand-surf was waiting patiently for the next storm-tide to propel it crashing forward.

I didn't hang around for long after I was paid by the film company and was soon on my bike again heading south towards the Draa Valley and Zagora. The route took me over a steep Anti-Atlas Mountain road and on to Agdz, where I stopped for a while to have a swim in a campsite pool before strolling through irrigated meadows that lay beneath shady palms. Further on, the road closely followed the contours of the oasis-cocooned, Draa-river valley and what should have been just an inconvenience and buzz-killer turned into an opportunity for replenishment.

My back tire deflated all of a sudden and I didn't have the tools to fix the puncture. I was confident that someone would soon come to my aid though, and I was right to be because a man on a push bike soon appeared and mended the puncture. That wasn't all he could do for me, I discovered to my delight as he reached into a pocket and drew out a compressed clod of golden hash pollen. Happy accident, yes I knew what that meant, since I'd run out of smoke and was on the lookout for some more. If his name was Mohammed and I was on my mountain bike, you could say Mohammed came to the mountain bike.

Timbuktoo
52 Days by camel

a roadside sign boasted on the outskirts of Zagora. Some journey, I thought, and one I was unlikely to take, ever. It was late when I arrived so I just booked into a city centre hotel and fell into my bed.

I explored the town centre next morning and was invited, or should I say corralled, into an artisan shop by an insistent, blue-turbaned trader. We drank mint tea while he talked about himself in a mixture of French and English, and emphasised his Touareg, nomadic ancestry. I didn't ask, but I'm pretty sure he would have said that given a choice between a saddle-sore inducing camel ride for 52 days and a cushy cushion in a shady shop, he'd have preferred the nomadic option.

I realised that it was in my interest to affect an interest in some less expensive object so he wouldn't have the opportunity to try selling me something more so, so I asked about a silvery pendant. Luckily, I'd chanced upon a Touareg cross, leather-strip-strapped necklace, which my nomad friend praised and recommended as a good choice. It looked like a flattened lizard with two big ears as it nestled on my chest, but I was glad to wear it since it was cheap and I could say thanks, but I'll see what else another time. A fresh batch of tourists ready-for-the-picking diverted my host's attention momentarily and I took advantage of the opportunity to make my escape back on to the street again.

I then had to escape the rays of a searing sun as I ran from palm-shade to palm-shade on my way back to my hotel. It was like a torrential downpour in reverse, with the furnacing sun trying to suck every bit of moisture from the Earth and its inhabitants below. The greedy star even coveted the thin film of sweat produced by my overworked glands in response to the solar onslaught. My plight didn't go unnoticed by an observant taxi driver, who tailed me from tree to tree and beckoned me to him. I pointed at the hotel across the street and then at myself and he nodded his head and drove off.

48 degrees Centigrade, now that was my new record I noted after a glance at the weather chart on the tv in the hotel foyer. An event taking place across the Atlantic ocean in the USA caused a slight stir in the everyday, entropical atmosphere of the town, It was the final of the soccer World Cup with Brazil and Italy as the opponents and, seeing as sight seeing was out of the question, I watched the game. It turned out to be a dull, defensive affair, which neither team deserved to win, and in a way neither did because Brazil won on penalties after extra time. Coincidentally, a Brazilian and an Italian watched along with me, and at full time the Brazilian was undemonstrative and the Italian was inconsolable.

The road leading south out of Zagora follows the Draa river as far as the town of M'hamid, where it comes to an end just a few miles short of the Algerian border, which can't however halt the progress of the Draa's own course as it makes its way into and disappears in the Algerian Sahara. I decided against following the southern desert-bound route as it was reputed to be featureless and unpopular with tourists, so I headed back to Ouarzazate, hoping to subsequently travel east towards Er-Rachidia and then south towards the renowned sand-dunes at Merzouga.

I wasn't long back in Ouarzazate, however, before I was approached yet again by the same agent who'd signed me up for the "Solomon and Sheba" film company. After a little persuasion, I said I was available to play the part of a member of the Jewish Council (Sanhedrin) along with other extras in a scene to be shot indoors at the studios on the outskirts of town. I wasn't tempted by the pittance offered for my services but was interested in a front row view of filming on a closed set and, spitefully some might say, wanted to see the expression on Gabrelli's face when we met again.

As it happened, the scene was due to be shot later on that same night and I was picked up in the town centre and driven along with a host of other extras on a bus to the studios. There I was once again decked out in pseudo-biblical fashion, not too dissimilar to the garb I wore as a cavalryman. I don't think members of the Sanhedrin Jewish Council wore turbans as we sported. In fact we should have worn mantilla-like shawls and who knew what else to play authentic parts.

Hours went by, waiting, waiting, waiting, until I was roused from a semi-stupor at around 5 o clock in the morning and told to go along with others into the hangar that housed the closed film set. Inside I was directed to stand along with the other members of the Jewish Council in a corner of a platform and told to wait for instructions. Maybe he hadn't noticed me or was too exhausted to care, but Gabrelli didn't confront me at first. He might even have chosen to ignore me if my turban hadn't come undone. I reached up and tried to stem the flow but only made it worse and that seemed to trigger a response from Gabrelli.

"How did he get in here?" he blurted out while simultaneously pointing at me, saying "I work hard, day and night, and this is what I get, sloppy extras that I've already gotten rid of being brought back to give me more headaches". He aimed a brush-off gesture my way, saying to anyone who cared to follow his order "get him out of here now. I refuse to carry on while he's still here".

Gratifyingly, no one seemed interested in carrying through the producer's edict. In truth, everyone on set was shagged tired, including Gabrelli, who was at least being paid well for his discomfort unlike most of the rest of us. Should've called for the cavalry, I advised in my imagination, but maybe they would have turned on him since he'd already dishonourably discharged two of them, including me. I couldn't think what to say for a while I was that groggy, but did ask him why he was so miserable and irascible and said that I didn't take kindly to bullies, big or small.

The wisdom of Solomon was not shown by the one named for the messenger archangel, but then how wise was Solomon really? The famous baby with two women claimants story was set to be filmed that night, but what was the truth behind the tale? One claimed, according to the bible, that her baby was stolen by the other, who replaced the live one with her own dead baby. Solomon then proposed to carve the baby in two, knowing all the while that the real mother would sooner give her child up to save its life than the alleged kidnapper. But how could he know for sure that his decision was correct?

Surely, I thought, Solomon could have come up with a less heavy-handed way of testing the women's feelings towards the baby. For instance, he, with all his wealth, could easily have asked one of his servants to place the baby in one of the panniers of a weighing scales while placing a measure of gold equal in weight to the baby on the opposite pannier. Then he could have asked the women which of them would prefer the baby and which the gold. Surely, I thought, the real mother would immediately opt for the baby while the impostor would at the very least have hesitated before choosing baby or gold.

Solomon didn't even need to be out of pocket once he'd awarded the custody of the baby to the woman who chose the baby without hesitation. The greedy one could justifiably be given nothing for her base behaviour and, even if the woman who claimed the baby wasn't its real mother, she obviously was likely to care for it more than the greedier one.

At a fundamental level, it's fair to ask about the origins of the Solomon/baby-judgement story itself. A theory has it that the story is a misrepresentation of an illustration created by a long dead, unknown artist, who took the truth about the true nature of his inspiration along with him to the grave. Many religious tales are based on the misinterpretation of ancient art after all?

Imagine, if you can, a painting showing a scene containing a figure with a crown on his head pointing towards a baby lying naked on a slab. A servant stands over the baby with a sword grasped firmly in his hand poised to carry out an order to kill, while two women look on. Biblical research has shown that it's more likely that the original artists meant to portray the annual ritual sacrifice of a baby surrogate in place of the Sun-God (Sol-omon)'s earthly representative, Solomon himself, so Solomon could live on and reign without incurring divine retribution for unoffered sacrifices. Were the two women in reality priestesses of the Moon-Goddess, who had offered the baby to Solomon, knowing full well that they would be allowed to dine on its grisly remains, flavoured with sprigs of laurel and ivy and washed down with a cocktail of hemlock and fly-agaric?

Solomon doesn't seem so wise if that was the case, or merciful. He didn't rate loose women very highly either, so why did he even bother to mediate their dispute. See in the bible where he said "you will be saved from the loose women, from the adventuress with smooth words…none who go to her come back again, nor do they regain the paths of life" and also "the lips of a loose woman drip honey and her speech is smoother than oil…in the end she is bitter as wormwood, sharp as a two-edged sword…her feet go down to death.." Does he sound like he could have cared less about such undeserving women?

Solomon seemed to be at his wisest, if you can believe that he said what he is reputed to have in the bible, when doubting the value of his own wisdom, as for example "there is nothing new under the sun…all is vanity…to know wisdom is a striving after wind…he who increases knowledge increases sorrow …I saw that the race is not to the swift, nor the battle to the strong, nor bread to the wise, nor riches to the intelligent, nor favour to the men of skill; but time and chance happen to them all…if the serpent bites before it is charmed, there is no advantage in a charmer…"

I never got to pass judgement but I did get a few shekels for my trouble and Gabrelli had made a fool of himself publicly. The lights of dawn seemed dim when I exited the spotlit hangar and I hurried towards the bus through the cool morning air. Third time lucky? I didn't wait around to see if I'd be hired again. Too much of a "good" thing etc.

Chapter 3.

I left town on the following day and headed north for the Marakech/Agadir intersection, where I turned east. The road to Boumaine du Dades passed through the Skoura Oasis, where mud-castle ksours and kasbahs clung to rocks like stranded coral creations beside sea-anemone-like date palms. There I turned left onto a by-road leading to the Dades Gorge and drove as far as Tamnalt, where I gazed in wonder at a natural rock formation called the "hills of human bodies", that looked like a petrified heap of limbs and torsos that once belonged to a race of giants. Eggshell, cayenne and shady-tropical-lagoon-green ksours and kasbahs perched on rock-mounds below could have been the petrified sandcastles of their children.
I returned to Boumaine and headed east to Tinerhir, where I turned left onto a road leading past the Todra Palmery as I travelled on towards the Todra Gorge. I forded a shallow river and.literally drove down Wall Street through a canyon with 100 foot high sheer cliff walls on both sides. Beyond the canyon the track led on to the High Atlas village of Imilchil, where an annual wedding market attracts prospective suitors in search of henna-dyed, scarved, jewellery-festooned brides, whose ululations shiver the clear mountain air.
I didn't fancy taking my chances on the steep mountain track since any breakdown could have left me stranded for the night, freezing and unsheltered, so I stayed in a hotel in the canyon. Rooms were a bit expensive, but I, along with some other "budget-minded" tourists were charged a little for sleeping on benches in a tented pavilion pitched in front of the main hotel building itself.
I returned to Tinerhir in the morning and then headed east again to Er-Rachida, where I went in search of a new back tyre for my moped in the medina. I noticed straight away that there was something different about the place, something unusual about the atmosphere, but it took me a little longer to come up with a good explanation for my own benefit. There were an awful lot of uniforms about, mostly soldiers, but why? The nearby Algerian border had to be the reason, I guessed, and most of the soldiers were conscripts who were used to police it. Waiters were mostly waitresses, that is women, unlike everywhere else I'd been in Morocco. Were the young conscripts being offered the company of unescorted young women as a way to keep their emotions occupied while they awaited possible military actions nearby or in Western Sahara to the south-west? Distractions for those who might be "in action" has always been a strategy employed by military types.
After I'd bought a new tyre I stayed the night in a dingy hotel, which seemed more like an army barracks than a civilian hotel, there were that many soldiers staying there. I expected to be woken up by a bugler and ordered to assemble on the parade ground. No thanks, I by the way refused to obey as I deserted early next morning and made a break for it.
I drove south through the Ziz valley and the Tafilalt Oasis on the old trade route that led to Timbuktu, where salt, gold and slaves were the transported commodities and stopped for a while at a spring-fed pool known as the "source bleu". I swam in cooling waters that gave life to the palm-groves of Meski and then drove on to Erfoud feeling refreshed.
It was a quiet place and would hardly have stuck in my memory if I hadn't slipped on the stairway of the hotel I was staying at and almost broke my arm. The cleaning lady smiled when I came tumbling down the just washed concrete steps and I can say that I wasn't too polite when I asked why she'd created the hazard. It didn't matter anyway since she couldn't understand a word I was saying. My tone of voice and grimacing obviously showed the hurt, mind you, but she just got on with her mopping in spite of signs of distress.
Everywhere I looked in Erfoud there were shops selling dark marble slabs with impressive, embedded fossils, in particular of giant spiralled ammonite shells that were homes to living creatures long ages ago when the Sahara desert was a seabed. Now the mostly circular and invariably highly polished slabs were destined for the homes of the wealthy in Morocco and

overseas, where they would be used as table-tops, objets d'arts to impress visitors. I could just imagine myself with one on the back of my moped, especially going round corners. Possibly two could have acted as wheels and I could have auditioned for a part in the Flintstones.

I left next day and drove to Rissani, ancient capital of the Tafilalt and last stop on the caravan routes south. It was hard to believe that such a nowhere place was used as a base by the Alaouite dynasty when they tried to extend their power northwards from a local religious academy (Zaouia) many centuries ago. Didn't the mountains of Galicia produce Franco and Castro and Stalin came from the Caucusus and Hitler from the Austrian Alps, so you could say that out of the way, hard living places are more likely to produce forceful personalities. More intolerant, now that's for sure!

The presiding monarch, Hassan II, is an Alaouite, but I'm pretty sure he doesn't visit the ancestral lands very often. I dare say he's too busy lounging in his palaces in Marakech, Agadir and so on. Still, I would confidently say that the people round about are inordinately proud of their royal heritage.

I wasn't some sort of royal groupie on a pilgrimage to the site of the origins of a dynasty, so I followed the road signs that pointed towards the giant sand dunes of Merzouga, which were the only sights that interested me. The route took me onto winding desert tracks, where I was glad of the protection afforded by my blue turban against the intense sunlight and occasional clouds of sand thrown up by passing vehicles. I paused to drink some fruit juice at an expensive hotel along the way and soon after I reached the Erg Chebbi, which is the highest sand-dune in Morocco. Its summit is over 500 feet above the surrounding desert, but is liable to shifting in storms as the sand-sea flows in enormous sand-waves across the Morocco/Algeria border. The fossilised remains of long-dead sea creatures and the skeletal remains of much more recently marooned terrestrial ones are the only anomalous objects likely to be discovered in all that sand, apart of course from humans and their constructs.

I parked my moped and waded into the soft sand at the base of the dune, thinking to myself that it was like paddling in the ebbing broken surf on an ocean strand threatened by a looming Tsunami sand-wave. It was just as well then for my sake that the sand-sea-scape was in still life.

The bullying Sahara thinks nothing of kicking mountainfuls of sand in (Charles) Atlas's face, but neither can ever gain the upper hand on the other as Mother Earth pushes the mountains up from below to replace rock eroded by the desert. You'd think the conditions would be too harsh for humans, but just like the sea-pirates who roamed the Coast of Barbary on the Atlantic Ocean west of the Atlas in search of rich pickings in bygone days, sand-pirates also stalked ships-of-the-desert sand-armadas as they sailed on the sand-sea, waiting for an opportune moment to ambush.

Nowadays, though, busloads of package tourists are led blinking and stumbling across the yielding sandy terrain, clicking cameras, unfinishing sentences, gasping for breath, mopping brows, wondering when they'll get back to their hotels again. Rich pickings hardly, but some more adventurous tourists go on camel treks in the desert, either for short spins or for overnight, sleep-beneath-the-stars, Arabian-nights-experience journeys.

Even after a short spell out in the open, I needed to retreat from the blazing sun's micro-waving rays, so I returned to my moped and drove on for a bit till I came upon a little tin-roofed, mud-walled bar. There I drank a cool bottle of orange juice while I tried to have a conversation with a couple of "homme bleu" Touaregs.

"How can you live in such a hard place?" I asked and one of the Touaregs looked straight at me with a facial expression that said more than any words could have. It seemed to say; another I-cant-take-the-heat, I-cant-stand-the-sand-in-my-shoes, I-need-a-shower, my-throat-hurts, temperate-lander. The desert is my habitat. You belong to lands of mist and ice. The

Erg Chebbi's flanged crescents seemed to be waving goodbye as I hurried off, wishing to get back to my hotel in Erfoud before sundown.

Next day I headed north through Er-Rachidia and then further northwards past the reservoir lake at Barrage Hassan Addakhil and into the Gorges du ZiZ (gazelle), where I followed the Ziz river on its course through a deep-gouged, sheer-cliff-sided, oasis canyon, past rosy-red Ksour mud-castles.

I even drove through the Atlas mountains inside the Tunnel Du Legionnaire, which was built by the occupying French army in the 1930s. I listened for a ghostly remain of a "Marseillaise" refrain but only heard my own humming version as I emerged out the other end. The town of Rich must have been hiding its opulence as I passed through on my way to the mountain pass at Tizi'n'Talrhmeht (she-camel) in the High Atlas.

I descended into Midelt, gateway to the Middle Atlas, and then drove on to Azrou through a cedar forest. Tall majestic trees lined either side of the road except for clearings, which offered glimpses of layered, undulating tree-waves careering through valleys and storm-tossed against mountain-sides. I stayed the night in a hotel in Azrou, where I bought two miniature cedar-wood busts of a Berber man and woman from a craftsman at his workshop in the medina. They were worth buying for the scent alone which reminded me of incense mingled with sandalwood.

Next day I headed south-west out of Azrou on a back-road to Khenifra through the cedar forest again, where I was lucky enough to come upon a troop of Barbary apes. I turned off the engine on my moped and stopped to take a good look at the gently loping apes, who seemed unalarmed by my presence and went about their business without any overt defensive display. I kept my distance as I knew that they were wild animals and not some tea-time chimpanzees. The frisson I experienced could only happen to a person encountering free living, wild animals, and though they were well used to seeing humans, I by the way apologised for my intrusion into their territory before moving on. A beautiful electric-blue, blackbird-like bird swooped by, flashing iridescent violet on an emerald background flecked with sunlit tan and fleshy bark slivers that subtly faded to shadows where the sunlight was obscured.

Beyond the forest the road meandered over mountains and down to a tree-sheltered lake, where I lunched amid scenery reminiscent of Mediterranean coastal mountain ranges before travelling on towards the source of the Oum er Rbia river. I strolled along a footpath past lean-to makeshift cafes and stalls on my way to a drip dripping rock pool, which was the source of a rocky mountain stream. It was hard to believe that I was walking by the side of the beginnings of one of Morocco's major rivers, but having travelled extensively in the region, I realised that "flood channel" was a more accurate description of the so called rivers I saw, which were mostly dried up wadis awaiting the next surge of flood waters.

Local traders made half hearted attempts to sell me something, but having dealt with the more persistent ones at the Cascades D'Ouzoud, I just brushed them off easily enough. I might have stayed the night nearby but none of the available hotels took my fancy so I drove on to Khenifra, where I found a room for the night in a hotel in the town centre

Next day I drove on to Beni Mellal and up towards the heights of the Middle Atlas on a road that sliced through cacti gardens and then down a side road to the afore mentioned Cascades D'Ouzoud. I soon met up with the campsite manager I'd met two years before and he brought me to a site sheltered by a roof made of floor mats. I pitched my tent and strung a hammock between two upright poles and listened to the sound of the river that flowed just a few yards away on its way to the fast approaching cataracts. Even though it was the height of summer the waterfalls themselves seemed as dramatic as they could be, whether viewed from below, looking through rainbow arc-slivers painted on fall-foam at a churning storm-cloud in a rock-pool cup, or from the side at the top, while stretching my neck out to look at a rolling wave disappearing into mist.

I walked along a path on a rock promontory high above the falls-fed canyon and caught sight of a group of Barbary apes, who were often to be seen roundabout the falls, where they were attracted by the lure of easy food pickings. I kept my distance and looked on as they scrambled over sinewy shrubs that reached out over the cliff's edge. Some of the juveniles hung from branch tips, swing-dangling from one hand above the chasm while extending the other out to grasp another branch-tip in a journey from branch to branch along a shrubbery flyover.

I went sight seeing on my moped after a couple of days and veered off down a dusty track prompted by a sign that pointed to a local river source. My heart missed a beat when a side-winding snake slithered across the track just yards in front of me. Who had the near escape, I'd say the snake was in more danger, but what if I'd fallen? At the source a few Moroccan tourists paddled in the clear waters of a pool, which was fed by springs issuing from a rock-vent and I cooled my own dusty feet in the refreshing waters before continuing with my tour. Another track led through a scrubby, spaghetti-western desert-scape down a winding track to a fortified little village, which was like a ghostly mirage with mud-walls enclosing termite-mound textured dwellings overlooked by feathery, date-palm crowns.

Back at the campsite after my day's journey, I decided that it was time to take to the road again, on towards palm-fringed Marakech. I'd travelled for over a thousand miles over the Atlas mountains and into the Sahara Desert and back into the Atlas again on my moped. I didn't fancy the return journey to Agadir, so I offered it for sale to the campsite manager, who could only offer me a third of the price I paid for it. I sold it to him anyway and a local official recorded the sale for legal reasons. At least, I thought, I didn't have to sell at the last minute and possibly for even less.

I bussed it to Marakech, where I stayed in a seedy hotel near the Djemaa El Fnaa with shuttered rooms facing a central courtyard shaded by the branches of a tall, slender tree. The clientele, who were just as seedy as the surroundings, included a drunken Irish-American novelist type and a young English couple trying to escape from their suburban strait-jackets. I bought a pair of leather sandals at a stall in the Djemaa on the following day and went sight seeing. I consulted a tourist map and strolled past the imposing Koutubia Minaret towards the Saadian Tombs, where filigreed, Arabic lattice-work adorned tiled crypts. Next up was the "El Badi" Palace, which was built during the reign of Ahmed El Mansour, who defeated the Portuguese army at the "battle of the three kings" at Ksar El Kebir around the end of the sixteenth century, but was subsequently, unfortunately, almost razed to the ground by Moulay Ismail.

It still looked a bit like a bomb site when I saw it, with dried-up sunken pools and unlived-in shells of rooms. I tried to visualise it at its most magnificent, but couldn't and paused instead for a moment to empathise shiveringly with the previous doomed inmates of a subterranean dungeon. Were the condemned prepared for a quick execution or were they subjected to torture and starvation in the course of a long, slow, agonising death? Surely, they were unfortunate enough to choose the losing side in a struggle for power or to be too closely related to someone who sought to eliminate perceived contenders for the power he coveted, I imagined.

The leather straps on my sandals began to eat into my bare toes, now there was a torture that could enhance my empathising as I left the palace behind and walked alongside a golf course, where the lush verdant fairways and manicured greens were in stark contrast to the dry-as-dust, sandy, Turner-haze-yellow, surrounding city-scape. Fore, I warned, as I watched a golfer play. Foreplay, I would have said to lovers a' wooing.

No pain, no gain, the saying has it, but since I had little to gain from further explorations except deeper welts, I decided to return to my hotel, where I exchanged the instruments of torture for my old flip-flops. On the way I visited the Mellah Jewish quarter, where very few actual practising Jews still lived, and bought some Berber-inspired necklaces strung with beaten metal baubles, tinged glass beads and arrowhead-shaped coral pieces. My favourite necklace had an embossed Touareg Cross pendant, which my Touareg friend in Zagora would surely have admired.

The present-day jewellery-makers learnt their craft from descendants of apprentices to the original Jewish craftsmen, whose descendants have mostly been deported or have emigrated, fleeing pogroms or escaping from the gradual, drip-dripping, tightening of restrictions upon religious and cultural freedoms and the ever increasing isolationism inflicted upon them by an exclusivist, mono-culturalist, nationalist majority.

One of the jewellery-makers actually accused me of behaving like a Berber when I tried to barter for a lower price. I was amused since I knew that I was nowhere near as pushy as the berbers I'd met in the Atlas mountains. It did make me think though, how once one source for stereotypical scapegoats has disappeared, people will look for replacements wherever they can. The jews were history all right, but the exclusivists needed a replacement and were quick to pour scorn on the people from the mountains even though many of their ancestors came to the city from there in the recent past.

Marakech enchants to begin with, but the spell is soon broken when you look for somewhere to eat and are overcharged for platelets of bland food served up in stalls in the Djemaa El Fnaa town square. Wander off up a side street and you could be in a French town centre or into the medina, where hustlers will offer to guide you out of the maze back to the Djemaa whether or not you've asked for assistance, and believe me you will get lost. I've had several encounters with such types and was sometimes able to give them the slip, but one in particular proved so persistent that I accepted his direction. He brought me to the Djemaa and as soon as I realised that I could make my own way back to my hotel, I gave him ten dirhams, which was about one Euro. I'd say it took him five minutes to lead me to the square, but he obviously thought that he'd saved my life or something. He swore at me and wished me ill, but outside in the public space he could do me no more harm. I glanced at an orange juice seller, who looked like he'd seen it all before. I guess he had more to fear from the hooligan than me.

I exchanged the claustrophobic cells of Marakech for the seaswept shores of Taghazoute campsite, where I rented a ready-pitched tent surrounded by a flimsy bamboo perimeter fence, which came with its own little succulent garden. I readjusted to beach-life, swimming daily in the sea, eating seafood at beachside restaurants, smoking joints in the privacy of my tent, relaxing, walking on the beach and stargazing. The surface of the ocean was a blue blanket with a bleached, frayed hem by day, illuminated spectacularly at sunset by a golden streak between sun and shore and subtly afterwards by a silver line cast by a giant-pearl, rising moon.

The Moroccan army didn't have to lay siege, but they did invade my territory in a way because the campsite manager asked me to vacate my tent so she could rent it to some Moroccan army officers on vacation. I could see why she wanted to suck up to the authorities and accepted the offer of a cheap rate in a 2-man tent rather than waging war. Maybe I should have advised them to rent a room in the village from my drunken, oppressive ex landlord, Said. I bet he would have been a quiet boy in that case.

I didn't fancy the cooped-up tent, so I decided to do some more touring in the little time I had left before my flight was due to depart from Agadir airport. I wanted to stay by the coast and not too far from Agadir, so I bussed it to the port of Essaouira, which is about a hundred miles to the north.

Unlike my previous visit 14 years before when I was destitute and suffering from dysentery and toothache, I could afford to stay in a pensione and felt fit. There was something missing though. Maybe my impoverished circumstances and the camaraderie engendered among travelling companions by a shared struggle for survival made me see things differently the first time I visited Essaouira. Were the natives friendlier then? It seemed to me that they were, and that the atmosphere in the town was less uptight.
Second time round I felt penned in by the massive Portuguese-built ramparts and lonely in a maze of dark alleyways echoing to the sounds of clip-clopping, sandaled feet. Down by the quayside I could dine on freshly cooked fish while looking out to sea beyond the jostling boats, but I never felt at ease served by grumpy cooks.
With little else to do and smoke all gone, I strolled about for a couple of days, along an ancient pier washed by crashing waves, above on ramparts and under archways, punctuated by glasses of mint tea and coffee sipped at tables at restaurants clustered round the main square.
Agadir felt more like home when I returned, but I was still glad to fly out of there back to Dublin. I needed a vacation from vacationing, you could say. I travelled by train as far as Rathmore in Kerry, where I was amazed to see a teletext report on a television in a bar saying that a plane travelling from Agadir to Casablanca had crashed in the Atlas Mountains.
On reflection, I realised that the crashed plane had departed just before my own flight and, what's more, that I'd seen some of the doomed passengers as they were making their way towards their last journey on this Earth. Lucky for me, I still had some journeys on this Earth to look forward to.

Part 4.

Fortnights.

Chapter 1.

Spring 2007.

March 3rd to 17th.

I flew from Dublin on a Sunways charter flight aboard a Royal Air Maroc plane on March 3rd and landed in Agadir airport after sunset. I blagged a ride in the Sunways' bus into town because I was afraid I'd be ripped off by a taxi driver, but I would have been better off with a taxi, I realised later. I was travelling flight only so I wasn't entitled to a bus ride to the expensive hotel where the package holidayers were to be dropped off, the bossy, sour Moroccan woman Sunways travel rep said, but she relented a bit and said I could come aboard for a fee of 10 Euros.
I didn't have any cash on me so I offered to give her the money when I reached the town centre, where I could get it from a cash point, and she grudgingly let me on, mumbling something about how my passage had to be paid for and she was liable to be charged for it. Maybe that was the case, but her graceless behaviour didn't help to endear her. Maybe she was diddled out of money in similar circumstances by other tourists previously, but she never told me she was.
Now, I thought, as I slid my debit card into the hotel ATM and pressed some buttons, I can pay the shrew and get on with my holiday, but nothing happened and it slid out again. I went out to the bus and told her that I needed to try some other ATMs because the hotel one wasn't coughing up, but she became even sourer and told me to hand in the money at the Sunways office when I got it. I asked for the address and went on my way, but where, oh where was I going to get any money?
A petit taxi driver moved in on me, no doubt sensing the opportunity for some business, and when I told him about my money problems I thought he would scarper. He obviously knew that the local ATMs weren't universally forthcoming, because he offered to drive me round to some ATMs at different banks, and what other choices did I have? I tried a few and had no success until, Eureka, an ATM at a WAFA bank or, as I called it, "a jar of waffles", which was a pun on its full title, poured forth what was beseeched.
I asked the sub Saharan taxi driver to take me to a cheap hotel and he asked if I wanted to buy some hash. I said "yes, please!" and offered him 30 Euros equivalent for a lump, which he initially said was twice the price. He handed it over anyway and dropped me off outside the Hotel Tamri near the Jardin Olhao Portuguese garden in the Talborjt district. I went inside and booked a room and smoked away the stresses of the journey.
I was looking forward to having a bite to eat at a beach restaurant when I boarded a bus bound for Taghazoute, my old haunt, but where were they, I puzzled, when I finally arrived at the scene. All was ruins, both restaurants and the friendly grocery store, but why? I asked at some stalls on the path to the campsite, but people seemed anxious as they replied evasively. I began to understand when someone said it had something to do with the King, but what right did he have? Every one seemingly, though all not in on the royal scheme could only see the destruction. Surely, I thought, he planned to develop the site. The Acropolis, it wasn't.
After a few days I bussed it to Banana Village and took a minibus taxi to Immouser through Paradise Valley. I walked to the Cascades and was surprised to see a local man dive into a pool from a height of about 50 or 60 feet. He expected some payment

for the feat even though I never asked him to do it, so I just gave him 5 dirhams and left him shivering as I made a quick exit.

I stayed the night in a pricey hotel for a cut-price rate of 30 Euros equivalent and drank a couple of beers purchased at the Uniprix supermarket in Agadir and smoked joints in my room. I watched TV for a while in a communal lounge, where a young man invited me to visit his family in the village, but I declined, saying I was too tired. Actually though, I didn't fancy the prospect of trying to avoid stumping up for some reason or other since my funds were limited, nor did I wish to attempt to make small talk with people who only ever spoke a language I knew so little of. An old Berber man came in and tutted disapprovingly when he saw a dancing woman on a music video on the TV. "Arab", he uttered, and not in a complimentary way. Now, if it was a camel, I bet he would have admired it.

On the return journey next day the driver of the past its best Mercedes taxi had to stop halfway up a hill to let the engine cool. I wondered how he got it up the mountain to begin with since the journey from Banana village to Immouser was nearly all uphill. The fare was only 5 Euros or so for about 30 miles and, though a taxi might carry up to 6 persons at once, normally they carry less and I'm sure that locals pay that much less than tourists. As for insurance, don't ask!

Disasters, or perceived ones, live longer in the memory than most enjoyable experiences, unfortunately, but can, in hindsight, seem humorous after a while. A dose of the shits is a common enough ailment in Morocco, I know, but I had an almighty dose after eating a fish paella in a renowned fish restaurant in Agadir. My stomach rumbled while I was walking about and I had to run into a public garden space and squat behind some bushes, and not a second too soon as my arse exploded. I shouldn't have gone to the cinema, I know now, because I shit myself while I was sitting there and had to leave in a hurry. Don't ask me what the film was called! Maybe "Gone with the wind" or "The turd man".

Back at my hotel, I stripped and showered and wanted rid of the excrementary evidence, so I stuffed my soiled trousers in a plastic bag and chucked it out the window, hoping to retrieve it later on and dispose of it properly. As it happened, the hotel proprietor was out on the street below when my offering came flying out of my window and he must have thought it fell out somehow because he retrieved it and brought it to me in my room. I accepted it sheepishly and tried to explain what happened, but he didn't bat an eyelid and I said thanks and threw it in a garbage bin on the street outside later.

I often ate at a restaurant near my hotel, where I was accosted once by the Moroccan travel rep who was so slow to let me on the bus when I arrived in Agadir. She asked me about the money I owed and I asked if I could get a ride back to the airport when I was leaving. She said it would cost me 10 Euros extra and I said I would pay it along with the initial fee when I visited the Sunways office to confirm my seat on the flight back to Dublin. That seemed to satisfy her, but she still looked awful grumpy as she went on her way again.

I paid my debt at the office a couple of days before leaving and arranged to be picked up at the package holidayers' hotel on the departure date. There was some news on the TV in the foyer that the Irish cricket team had just beaten Pakistan in the World Cup. Wonders will never cease, I thought as I arrived back in Dublin on St. Patrick's day and exchanged cricket bats for shillelaghs.

Chapter 2.

Spring 2014.

March 22nd to April 5th.

I flew from Dublin to Agadir on board an Aer Lingus flight on March 22nd 2014. Again I made trouble for myself where I could have avoided it by accepting a ride from a man with a minibus, who seemed a reasonable choice at the time. I would advise tourists to take a taxi because there's a notice near the rank advertising the going rate for the trip to Agadir town centre and you can insist on paying it.
The man with the minibus had an official air about him, which should have alerted me, but what was he on the lookout for if he was interested in me, I couldn't figure. If I was puzzled for a while, the mystery soon cleared somewhat when we got to the town centre and I was charged 20 Euros for the ride. It was a good bit more than the official taxi fare and the taxi driver wouldn't have asked so many questions.
I booked into the Hotel Central just a short walk from the hotel I stayed in in 2007 and walked to the beach front. Again I should have known better but I asked a couple of likely lads sitting on a wall if they knew anyone with hash to sell. Almost immediately I was joined by a prospective dealer, who hurried me along towards the shade of a palm tree, where he showed me a little dark rectangular plastic-wrapped piece and asked for the equivalent of 70 Euros. I gave him 30 and he didn't stay around to haggle. I soon found out why when I unwrapped the piece of, what it was I can't say, but what it wasn't I can say was hash.
I was mighty annoyed, but at least I only gave away 30 Euros and in all my time in Morocco it was the first time I was ripped off for smoke, so I just wrote the loss off in my mind as a form of local tax. As if, you could say, but I knew a shop in the market where I was sure to score the real thing, so I only had to wait till early next day.
I'd bought some in 2007 from a contact of the shopkeeper and I hoped for a similar outcome as I entered the shop and made some enquiries. The server knew allright and he made a phone call to summon the dealer, who tried to sell me a lot more than I wanted understandably. I told him I was only going to be in town for a couple of weeks so I just needed enough for that, so he sold me about 10 grams for 60 Euros equivalent. It was overpriced by local standards, I know, but it worked.
I bussed it to Taghazoute in the afternoon and swam in the ocean. I looked over at the place where the restaurants once stood and wondered why they were demolished if there weren't any plans to replace them. Maybe the powers invoked some by-law that was circumvented by the developers who built the restaurants to begin with and ordered the demolition. And now, what do we have instead? An empty lot where no private developer wants to invest in since someone might decide that any buildings should be demolished at a later date.
I returned to Paradise Valley on a day trip after a few days and took a minibus-taxi as far as Immouser. I drank a coffee in the forecourt of the expensive Hotel de Cascades and chatted with the proprietor, who also owned the Hotel Sindibad in Agadir. With all his wealth he seemed uptight, but don't most wealthy people anyway? In Europe, of course, it's a lot easier to ignore the poverty, which is mostly confined to slums in cities, but in Morocco you can't miss it, whether on city streets or market alleys or down by the beach. You needn't look too close, if that helps.

The hotel gardens were well kept and the views were picture postcard, but I felt constrained by the artificiality. A bird perched on a branch above and then took flight off over an Italianate railing and a cliff that descended over 50 feet towards a swimming pool before disappearing into the wilds. I took my cue from it and went walkabout, on to the waterfall, which was quiet and then back to the village, where I was approached in a restaurant by a young Bin Laden lookalike, who spoke to me in an American accent. A 4x4 jeep with some showoffy, loud western tourists drove by, but he didn't seem bothered. He seemed bored indeed, possibly because he was more inspired by the fashion than the faith of fundamentalist Islam.

In the 2nd week I decided to go on tour to Marakech and on to Ouarzazate and then back to Agadir. I stowed most of my luggage at the hotel and bussed it to Marakech, where I stayed in a cheap hotel near the Djemaa El Fnaa for a couple of days. It was unseasonably cold with massing grey clouds, so it felt even more claustrophobic than usual, and self-appointed guides haunted my every step whenever I ventured into alleys, so nothing new there, I judged. Why then had I returned to Marakech, I asked myself before reminding myself that I was en route to Ouarzazate in the desert by way of the Atlas Mountains, and boy was it some trip.

It was only 8 degrees C when the rickety bus left Marakech behind and headed for Ouarzazate on slippery, icy roads. Snow was falling lightly on an Artic scene alongside and above as melting waters drained into wadis down below, carrying eroded sediments that coloured streams brown and translucent green and soupy pink. Once I saw an eagle gliding in a valley beneath and reckoned that the snow helped to highlight the presence of possible prey. I shuddered when I realised that I was just a slip away from ending up as a feast for a vulture down there. The bus was old and dilapidated and most likely inadequately serviced, but the driver was used to its ways and to the dangerous conditions on the route, I told myself, fingers crossed. Indeed, I was probably safer than the pampered passengers on top of the range, modern coaches we met coming the other way, because their drivers weren't used to the prevailing conditions.

Ouarzazate was chilly in comparison to the last time I'd visited, but still mild enough when I arrived. I booked into the Hotel Royal and was looking forward to sampling the atmosphere, but what atmosphere, I soon asked myself? In 1994 there was a lot of film making going on locally and the place had a cosmopolitan feel to it with people from many different backgrounds and nationalities roaming about, but where were they in 2014? I intended to visit the film studios on the edge of town but there wasn't any filming going on, so I gave it a skip.

In fact, I was that bored that I planned to leave next day and bought a bus ticket for a bus to Agadir, that was due to leave on the following day. I missed it because the clock was brought forward an hour overnight and noone told me, so I had to stay an extra day. I'd only brought a small amount of smoke, having left the remainder behind in my luggage in Agadir, and that was gone, so I bought a few cans of lager at a supermarket and drank them on the roof of my hotel while sunning myself.

When I explained what happened, the bus ticket collector accepted my out of date ticket without a murmur and I was on my way back again to Agadir. I fancied a bit of luxury for my last couple of days, so I retrieved my luggage from the Hotel Central and upgraded to the Hotel Tour De Sud on the Avenue President Kennedy. I got a room on the third floor with a small balcony and a TV and, though the TV was full of rubbish and the view wasn't so panoramic, it was airy and bright and had a fuctioning en suite shower and toilet.

Cans of lager from the Uniprix and joints helped me to settle in to my room and I resumed my routine, which included walks along the beach front promenade, where I ate snacks and drank some more beer at the Café Jour Et Nuit. Near to my hotel, I sometimes breakfasted and dined at restaurants in the Place Lahcen Tamri and drank coffees in cafes, where there always seemed to be a soccer match on the TV.
On the day of my departure, I bussed it to Inezgane, where I looked for a bus to the airport, but all enquiries led me round in circles and I took a taxi instead. The driver asked me for less than 10 Euros, so I gave him a tip when he dropped me off, and it wasn't "exercise regularly and eat healthily!".
Who should I see in the airport, only the grumpy Moroccan travel rep, who'd given me such grief in 2007. I felt like going up to her and asking if she'd got her money, and not in a friendly way, but I didn't bother. She was busy charming her charges and who was I to break the spell?
I flew back to Dublin and arrived in the dead of night on April 5th.

Chapter 3.

Autumn 2015.

October 11th to 25th.

I flew from Dublin to Marakech on a Ryanair jet on October 11th and got a taxi into the town centre for about 6 Euros. The Djemaa El Fnaa was bustling but not overcrowded, so I found the hotel I'd stayed in the year before easily enough. Unfortunately, no room with an outward looking window was available, but I booked into one with an inward looking window anyway since I only intended staying for one night. I liked the design, though ex-cons from some American penitentiaries might not have because it reminded me of some prisons I've seen in films. A central square courtyard was enclosed by a four storey building with interior balconies on three sides at each level and connecting stairs. Unlike the prisons, however, the inmates were free to come and go and the courtyard wasn't an exercise pen for edgy psychotics. Instead, people lounged on armchairs and sofas in a garden beneath a 4 storey high ceiling. There was even an open air viewing area on the top level with a table for those who wished to eat food dished out from a hatch on a kitchen which was closed any time I saw it. The view was poor enough, just more squares extending out in every direction in a monotonous, shadowy grid, and we weren't even supposed to smoke a spliff or puff a pipe according to a warning notice. As if the place wasn't dreary enough already, and even beer was banned.

I bussed it to Agadir next day and booked into the Hotel Tour De Sud. Then it was off to score some hash, which I got in the market. I fancied a spell by the beach, so I went looking for a place to stay in or near Taghazoute, but could only find overpriced, overcrowded rooms. One house seemed more like a rundown squat than a hotel and, as the proprietor led me up a narrow stairs and told me to crouch down to avoid hitting my head off the ceiling I felt sure that the price would be cheap. He showed me into a cramped room with two mattresses on the floor and asked if I was prepared to share with a young couple and I said, "no thanks! Have you any rooms for one?" He nodded and brought me to an even smaller room with a mattress on the floor and, though I didn't like it, I asked how much anyway. The answer was about twice what I was paying already in the, for me, relatively expensive Tour De Sud, and how could he get away with it, I wondered as I made my excuses and left.

I made some enquiries in Banana village, but couldn't find an affordable room, so I went looking for a place to swim. I'd noticed on the bus that the beach just south of Banana Village was deserted and I soon found out why when I got a closer look. A young man invited me over to a solitary makeshift café perched on a sand dune above, but I just said "where can I swim?" while looking on appalled at the plastic waste swirling in the waves. A lone surfer, who must have been given the wrong directions, seemed in danger of death by lamination.

And yet I discovered a beach on the north side of town at a place called Imourane which was clean and the only plastics I could see were surf-boards, which were many and had to be avoided. There were several restaurants overlooking a crescent shaped bay, which was bordered on one side by the Roche De Diable (Devil's rock), which helped to funnel a constant procession of mighty waves onto a beach eaten out of the volcanic, rocky shore. No wonder then that the surfers loved the place, and swimmers too, who like to dive through walls of water.

Paradise Valley was just a few miles inland and when I visited a few days later I looked forward to unspoilt scenery. It had been raining for a few days and the minibus taxi from Banana Village could only take me as far as a section of the road littered with rocks washed off the mountains. A few hundred yards away on the other side of the slide another minibus taxi driver beckoned to me, so I paid the driver of the taxi I'd come in and walked briskly through the genuinely "rocky road" towards the other taxi. I intended originally to go on to Immouser, but the driver said the road was dodgy and advised me to visit a tourist trail, which was only a mile or so up the road. Other tourists in the taxi said they were going there, so I decided to join them, especially when I found out that an old man, who I mistook for a native because he was so tanned and inconspicuous, was from County Cork like myself.

I drank an orange juice at a makeshift restaurant on the roadside before walking on a rocky mountain path along with the other tourists and a couple of locals hired by the old man to prepare a picnic. We descended towards a canyon where the path followed the contours of the river as we wound our way down to the riverside. Usually the waters run clear and whispering, but after the recent deluge they were the colour of guava juice and whooshing along.

The scene as I scanned the surrounds from a rocky height was out of Paradise indeed, with low growing pines, argan trees, tall, leggy date palms and a strawberry juice waterfall, but you couldn't filter out those plastic bottle mounds. A few waste disposal bins could have solved the litter problem, but it might take a lot more to make the litterers appreciate the fragility of nature. At least the pollution was visible and could be easily got rid of, unlike industrial waste from manufacturing processes or mining or road building and such.

The old man invited me to join him and his charges for a tajine in a simple restaurant near the river and I gratefully accepted. He said he had a farm near Buttevant in north Cork, but preferred to live in a house he bought near Taghazoute with a view of the sea. The other tourists, a young German couple and a young Dutch man with two young Dutch girls were staying at the old man's house as paying guests seemingly, but apart from one of the Dutch girls, I found them standoffish. The old man though was like a breath of fresh air to their stuffy auras as he happily recounted his exploits while under the influence of ecstacy tablets and cocaine. The middle Europeans shifted uncomfortably as I complained about the poor quality of the hash peddled on the streets of Agadir compared to the stuff I'd bought on earlier visits, and the Dutch man in particular insisted that he didn't smoke dope. Laid back Dutch indeed, I thought I'd met the exception to the rule, but on reflection I remembered those snooty Amsterdamers, who looked down their noses at dope tourists.

The old man moved on to religion as he complained about the muslim infighting, saying that the factions, whether Shia or Sunni couldn't decide between them what Muhammad represented. I agreed and said that the catholic/protestant Christian conflict was similar. The Dutch man then said we should respect each others' religious beliefs. And the lack of them if you don't believe there's a god to begin with, I added. He must have been brought up strict and terrorised into acceptance, but then so was I, at least until I began to think for myself.

An odd coincidence occurred to me later when I recalled the old man's story about the actor Jonathan Rhys Meyer, who'd stayed at the old man's house in Cork for a while. Seemingly he was trying to escape from some domestic problems. Meyer played King Henry VIII in a TV series. Now there was a man who would be God, at least in the safety of his palaces far from battlefields and crusades.

Oisin, the celtic hero came to mind as I watched the old man lift a fallen rock from the road on the way back. Oisin was on horseback though according to the myth and destined to live forever in the Land of the Young until he leant over and tried to lift a rock off the ground in answer to a challenge. The belt on his saddle snapped and he fell to the ground and instantly became an old man. I might have urged my friend to run after his horse, but instead I advised him to leave the clearing to the locals, who could make a few dirhams from the activity.

A couple of days later I left the Hotel Tour De Sud as I tried to cut costs. I stayed in two cheap and nasty hotels before I found the Hotel Diaf, which was cheap and cheerful. At least I had a room to shelter in unlike a homeless woman, who slept on the street just opposite my window. I wondered why the ones with the means or the power over resources didn't do anything to help her and the other destitutes who roamed the streets. Too much "Inshallah!", I'd say, and not enough "will of the people".

A pair of dealers left me exasperated, as one approached me on the street and I eventually bought a little but only after he made a show of his greed and whinged about the risks he was taking. At least the smoke was some bit effective unlike a bit I got from the dealer in the market who'd already sold me some pretty ok stuff. I was annoyed, and why wouldn't I be, since I'd already brought custom his way. Fat chance, I thought, that I'd be recommending him to friends who might visit Agadir in the future. Zero zero really lived down to its name with that cod-hash.

I bussed it back to Marakech on March 25th and had just about enough money to afford a taxi to the airport, where I boarded a flight bound for Dublin.

Printed in Great Britain
by Amazon

40047665R00046